Timeless Top 10 Travel Guides

Hong Kong

Hong Kong's Top 10 Hotel Districts, Shopping and Dining, Museums, Activities, Historical Sights, Nightlife, Top Things to do Off the Beaten Path, and Much More!

By Tess Downey

Copyrights and Trademarks

All rights reserved. No part of this book may be reproduced or transformed in any form or by any means, graphic, electronic, or mechanical, including photocopying, recording, taping, or by any information storage retrieval system, without the written permission of the author.

This publication is Copyright ©2017. Nevada. All products, graphics, publications, software and services mentioned and recommended in this publication are protected by trademarks. In such instance, all trademarks & copyright belong to the respective owners. For information consult www.NRBpublishing.com

Disclaimer and Legal Notice

This product is not legal, medical, or accounting advice and should not be interpreted in that manner. You need to do your own due-diligence to determine if the content of this product is right for you. While every attempt has been made to verify the information shared in this publication, neither the author, neither publisher, nor the affiliates assume any responsibility for errors, omissions or contrary interpretation of the subject matter herein. Any perceived slights to any specific person(s) or organization(s) are purely unintentional.

We have no control over the nature, content and availability of the web sites listed in this book. The inclusion of any web site links does not necessarily imply a recommendation or endorse the views expressed within them. We take no responsibility for, and will not be liable for, the websites being temporarily unavailable or being removed from the internet.

The accuracy and completeness of information provided herein and opinions stated herein are not guaranteed or warranted to produce any particular results, and the advice and strategies, contained herein may not be suitable for every individual. Neither the author nor the publisher shall be liable for any loss incurred as a consequence of the use and application, directly or indirectly, of any information presented in this work. This publication is designed to provide information in regard to the subject matter covered. Neither the author nor the publisher assume any responsibility for any errors or omissions, nor do they represent or warrant that the ideas, information, actions, plans, suggestions contained in this book is in all cases accurate. It is the reader's responsibility to find advice before putting anything written in this book into practice. The information in this book is not intended to serve as legal, medical, or accounting advice.

Foreword

Hong Kong is one of Asia's key cities that stood the test of time and an essential part of the 21st century. As soon as you arrived in this magnificent city, you will find yourself in awe not just because of its different tourist attractions but also because of its evolving culture and dynamic heritage that had been passed on for generations.

Immerse yourself in the city's past through its different arts and culture festivals, historical monuments, and delicate dishes; experience what Hong Kong can offer today through its various tourist destinations, vibrant nightlife and amazing people; prepare yourself to be a part of its future as it becomes one of the capital financial and trading cities that is going to shape the world we live in.

Embark on a fun-filled journey that will last you a lifetime, own every second that Hong Kong could offer and learn why this city is known as "the gateway of the east and west," just like many of the greatest traders and tourists that came before you.

Table of Contents

Hong Kong 1

Introduction 1

Chapter One: Hong Kong Overview 5

    Hong Kong in Focus 6

    A Brief History of Hong Kong 8

    Hong Kong's Language, People and Culture 11

Chapter Two: Travel Essentials 15

    Immigration and Visas 16

    Seasons 30

Chapter Three: Getting In and Around Hong Kong 31

Chapter Four: Hotels and Accommodations 43

    1. Central (Hong Kong Island) 45

    2. Wan Chai 47

    3. Tsim Sha Tsui (TST) 49

    4. Causeway Bay 51

    5. Mong Kok 53

    6. Sheung Wan 55

    7. Lantau Island 57

    8. Peng Chau Island 59

    9. Lamma Island 61

    10. Stanley Village 62

Chapter Five: Shop and Dine 65

    1. Tang Lung Street 66

    2. Nga Tsin Wai Road 68

    3. Nathan Road 69

    4. Lan Kwai Fong 71

    5. Canton Road 73

    6. Hung Hom 74

    7. Percival Street 76

    8. Lung Kong Road 77

    9. Stanley Road 78

    10. Sai Kung 80

Chapter Six: Tourist Spots in Hong Kong 83

    1. Victoria Peak 84

    2. Hong Kong Disneyland 86

3. Hong Kong Ocean Park 88

4. Jumbo Kingdom (Aberdeen Harbour) 90

5. Avenue of Stars 91

6. Hong Kong Museum of History 92

7. Clock Tower 94

8. Ngong Ping 360 96

9. Golden Bauhinia Square 99

10. Victoria Harbour 100

Chapter Seven: Temples in Hong Kong 103

1. Po Lin Monastery (Tian Tan Buddha) 104

2. Ten Thousand Buddhas Temple 106

3. Man Mo Temple 108

4. Che Kung Temple 110

5. *Chi Lin Nunnery and Nan Lian Garden* 112

6. Fung Ying Seen Koon 114

7. Kwan Kung Pavilion 116

8. Seven Sisters Temple 117

9. Golden Flower Shrine 119

10. Hau Wong Temple 121

Chapter Eight: Interacting with Hong Kong 123

    1. Star Ferry Ride 124

    2. Duk Ling Ride 127

    3. Hong Kong Space Museum 129

    4. Hong Kong Cultural Centre 130

    5. Lin Heung Tea House 132

    6. Madame Tussauds Hong Kong 134

    7. Hong Kong Wet Land Park 136

    8. Hong Kong Museum of Art 138

    9. Yau Ma Tei Theatre 139

    10. Arts in the Park Mardi Gras 141

Chapter Nine: Nightlife in Hong Kong 143

    1. Symphony of Lights 144

    2. Victoria Harbour Square Cruise 146

    3. Aberdeen Harbour Night 148

    4. Temple Street Night Market 149

    5. Heli-Tour in Hong Kong 151

6. Lan Kwai Fong Bars and Pubs..153

7. Western and Chinese Night Clubs...............................154

8. Happy Valley Race Course 156

9. Opera House Hong Kong..158

10. Intercontinental Infinity Pools 159

Chapter Ten: Off Hong Kong's Beaten Path........................161

1. Tai O Fishing Village...162

2. Repulse Bay 164

3. Dragon's Back 166

4. Dialogue in the Dark 167

5. The Beach with the Buffalos...169

6. Mui Wo Clam Digging 171

7. Kadoorie Farm 172

8. Mai Po Nature Reserve 174

9. Hong Kong UNESCO Global Geopark 176

10. Hoi Ha Wan Marine Park 178

Quick Travel Guide 181

1. Hong Kong Quick Facts...182

2. Transportation 183

    Points of Entry in Hong Kong 183

    Transportation Services in Hong Kong 184

3. Travel Essentials 184

Immigration and Visas 184

PHOTO REFERENCES 191

REFERENCES 205

Introduction

There had been a lot of confusion with tourists when it comes to Hong Kong, the most common question is – is it a country or a city? Is it part of China? Perhaps one of the funniest questions in Google about Hong Kong is this: Is Hong Kong Chinese?? I don't know how Google responded to that one.

Introduction

One Country, Two Systems – that is what Hong Kong is all about. It's not a separate country even if it is isolated in mainland China but it's an independent city granted with a high degree of autonomous status by the People's Republic of China, which means that it has its rule of law, enjoys free trade, has freedom of speech and is an independent capitalist system (so yes – Hong Kong is Chinese after all!).

Hong Kong is the center of international trade in the East since the early 20th century up until today and will most likely still be in the next few years. According to locals, the constant thing about this city is change. Its ability to adapt and thrive in changing times without abandoning entirely its historical roots is what makes Hong Kong the best of both worlds.

Whether this is your first time to visit the culture-driven city of Hong Kong, or if this is one of the several trips you have made to this busy city, there's always something new and different to see. Whether it's the history, the sights, the entertainment, the feasts, the food, or the people - a trip to Hong Kong is always a worthy experience.

There is something for everyone - whether you're a history buff, an entrepreneur trying to learn how business works, an outdoors person looking for an adventure,

Introduction

someone who appreciates arts and even martial arts, or one who just loves to eat Chinese food, Hong Kong's got it all for you!

In this book, you will learn the basic things you need to know about Hong Kong – its location, its people, its language, culture and seasons. You will also be given information regarding your travel needs, and of course an overview of the top tourist attractions, hotels and food places as well as hidden facets of the city to meet your thirst for exploration.

So what are you waiting for? Get ready to pack your bags, your passport, and your pocket money! Let's set out for one of the most exciting places in the world. Adventure is out there!

Introduction

Chapter One: Hong Kong Overview

Before your plane lands on one of the most must-see cities in the world, it is essential to know intricate details of what you're about to deal with. Hong Kong is a big city, and if it is your first time to travel here, you might want to consider discovering facts about this awesome place, so that you know what to expect before you go about in your itinerary and to avoid getting into trouble. In this chapter, you will be provided with an overview of Hong Kong – its city, language, culture, people, and history.

Chapter One: Hong Kong Overview

If you have enough knowledge about these things, you will not just enjoy and appreciate the city but also get to be prepared for a different kind of adventure!

Hong Kong in Focus

Hong Kong is strategically located on the southeast coast of China specifically in the South China Sea and at the mouth of Pearl River Delta. The city's location is what makes it as the portal of the east and west, and is considered as one of the world's cosmopolitan cities.

After the First Opium War in 1842, Hong Kong was ceded and leased to Great Britain. The Stonecutter's Island

Chapter One: Hong Kong Overview

and Kowloon Peninsula together with the other 235 islands or New Territories nearby were also turned over to the British. Being the center of international trade especially back in the day, you will get to discover stories of European traders, powerful dynasties, sea pirates, and how the city became a new hub for manufacturing, which boosted its economic and industrial power during the 20th century.

In the past few years, Hong Kong became the gateway in accessing one of the world's largest market and economy – China. The city adapted to the economic changes of mainland China and transformed its role yet again by becoming a service-based economy in the 21st century.

As mentioned earlier, locals in Hong Kong believed that the only thing constant in this city is change but its roots remain active and its spirit indomitable because of the rich culture and heritage that has been passed on for generations.

On July 1, 1997, the Chinese government made Hong Kong autonomous. The principle of "One Country, Two Systems" turned the city into a Special Administrative Region of the People's Republic of China.

Chapter One: Hong Kong Overview

A Brief History of Hong Kong

Before Hong Kong reached this full autonomy status and before it became the city that it is today it had gone through different phases and major changes; let's have a quick look at what went down in its history.

700 BC — A floating community was established by early Chinese fishing communities

50 BC — Hong Kong became part of mainland China

AD 960 – 1500s — Different clans settle in the region and also began building walls around their villages to protect them against pirates

1514 — A base was built in Tuen Mun by Portuguese traders.

Early 1800s — Trading between Chinese merchants and British merchants began. The British exchanged opium for silver, silks, and spices

1840 – 1842 — Opium Wars began in China as a result. The Qing Dynasty eventually lost to the

Chapter One: Hong Kong Overview

	British forces; Hong Kong was surrendered to Britain. .
1860	The Stonecutters Island and Kowloon region were also turned over to Great Britain
1898	Hong Kong and the New Territories were leased to Great Britain which turned it into a trading port for 99 years.
1910	In China, the railway connecting Kowloon and Canton is completed.
1911 –1949	Hong Kong population increased due to the flocking of refugees from mainland China who was caught up with the country's political warfare.
1941 – 1945	The city was under the Japanese Occupation during World War II.
1950 – 1970s	The textile and light manufacturing industries were at an all-time high because of Chinese immigrants. Hong Kong began exporting goods around the world.

Chapter One: Hong Kong Overview

1980s	The city was included in the top 10 economies especially in Asia and became one of the international financial capitals of the world.
1984	The Sino-British Joint Declaration was signed by China and Britain.
1997 (July 1)	Hong Kong becomes a Special Administrative Region of the People's Republic of China.
1998	The Hong Kong International Airport is named one of the Top 10 Construction Achievements by the Construction Industry Manufacturers Association (CIMA).
2008	The 2008 Equestrian Olympic and Paralympic Games were co-hosted by Hong Kong.
2011	The national list of intangible culture under the UNESCO convention included four of Hong Kong's festivals which are Cheng Chau Bun Festival, Tai O Deities Parade, Tai Hang Fire Dragon Dance, and

the Yu Lan Ghost Festival of the Hong Kong Chiu Chow Community.

2015 – present   Hong Kong continues to become an international business center in the world and in Asia. Its rich culture and heritage continues to flourish more than ever.

Hong Kong's Language, People and Culture

As soon as you step foot in this city, you will be immediately exposed to a variety of Asian and European languages even if the vast population are speaking in

Chapter One: Hong Kong Overview

Chinese – thanks to its rich blend of colonial history and international affairs. Being the gateway of the east and the west, Hong Kong's spirit is that of an Asian with a Western touch. In this section, you will learn more about the kind of people you are going to mingle with, the culture that surrounds the city and the language that binds it all together.

Chinese

Mandarin is China's official dialect; however around 85% of people who live in Hong Kong speaks Cantonese. You might want to try to at least learn a few Cantonese or Mandarin phrases and words before you set out in Hong Kong for you to connect better with the locals. Other Chinese dialects are also spoken in the city such as Hakka, Taishanese and Teochiu. Always keep that handy dandy English – Chinese dictionary or Google's Cantonese/Mandarin translator right in your pocket!

English

Can't speak Chinese? No worries! Since Hong Kong's establishment as the portal for international trade, the city's people were practically raised to also speak the universal language in the world. English is widely spoken in Hong Kong and it is the preferred language in the business and financial industry, the government and also its tourism sectors.

You won't have any problem understanding the city because all of the official signs, public announcements, and most menus in restaurants are bilingual. Communication will not be a major issue because the locals especially people like taxi drivers, policemen, tourism employees and most of its natives are competent in speaking in English.

Multiculturalism

As what you may have noticed, Hong Kong is flexible when it comes to tradition and innovation. The level of cultural tolerance in this city is reflected with the use of different languages, dialects and its practice of different religions and beliefs. Hong Kong is a hub of Christian churches, Muslim mosques, Jewish Synagogues as well as Buddhist, Taoist and Sikh temples.

Its distinctive contemporary culture is a mixture of ancient traditions and present innovations; only in Hong Kong can you see elderly men still playing old Chinese board games using smartphones and digital tablets, and where marvelous modern architectures and skyscrapers are designed to meet the standards of *feng shui* masters.

Chapter One: Hong Kong Overview

Chapter Two: Travel Essentials

Now that you have learned several things about Hong Kong and already have general knowledge of the city, the next thing for you to learn about and accomplish before actually going there is the travelling requirements or traveller's info.

The travel requirements and some basic reminders in planning your trip to this city are essential in order for you to have a wonderful experience and not get into trouble especially in immigration and customs.

In this chapter, you will learn what you need to do for you to be able to travel to Hong Kong, things you need to bring and be aware of, the different transportations and

Chapter Two: Travel Essentials

ports of entry in and out of the city as well as essential information for first time travellers such as money, communication.

Immigration and Visas

Just like other countries, a valid and updated passport is required for all visitors to the city. Your passport should be valid for at least one month after your period of intended tour or stay in Hong Kong; on the other hand, people who have been regarded as a stateless person must have at least two months of passport validity after the period of intended stay.

Chapter Two: Travel Essentials

For tourists in general, you do not need a visa to enter the city of Hong Kong. Depending on nationality, visitors can stay for one up to 180 days without a visa.

You can check the nearest Chinese embassy in your area if you are unsure of your status. For further info regarding visa and passport requirements, please check the Immigration Department website at <http://www.immd.gov.hk/eng/>

As of now, only Indian nationals can visit the city for not more than 14 days without a visa as long as they have a valid travel document. Visa will be required for Indians who wants to stay in the Hong Kong for more than 14 days. Visit the Chinese Embassy for more details.

Travel Pass for Business Travellers

If you are a businessman who frequently visits Hong Kong, you may apply for the Hong Kong Special Administrative Region Travel Pass. This pass is intended to provide business travelers with a simplified and quick immigration procedure as long as they have valid passports and has an entry permit to do business in Hong Kong. Here are the eligibility criteria set by Hong Kong's immigration office if you want to avail a travel pass:

- Must have a primary purpose or need to visit Hong Kong on a frequent basis

Chapter Two: Travel Essentials

- Must have previously visited Hong Kong at least three times in a year before application. Visits to mainland China or Macau is not included
- Another option if in case the first two doesn't apply is that the Director of Immigration must be fully convinced and satisfied that your visits to the city may bring significant benefits economically.
- Business Traveller Pass holders may use Hong Kong residents' counters for simplified immigration clearance procedures.

The downloadable application form and further information on how to acquire the pass can be found on the Immigration Department website at <http://www.immd.gov.hk/eng/>.

Frequent Visitor e-Channel

If you would like to always travel to Hong Kong as a tourist, you can also apply for a Frequent Visitor Pass using computerized self-service e-Channels. Acquiring this kind of pass can provide a quick and easy clearance for you or your family at the immigration. Here are the eligibility criteria set by Hong Kong's immigration office if you want to avail a Frequent Visitor Pass:

- Must be 18 and above

Chapter Two: Travel Essentials

- Must hold a valid travel document or a valid multiple visit visa

- Must hold one of the following documents: HKSAR Travel Pass or APEC Business Travel Card with 'HKG' printed on the reverse side. (You may inquire with your airline regarding the Hong Kong International Airport Frequent Visitor Card Frequent Flyer Program membership card)

- Another option you can take if in case you don't have the documents mentioned about is first, there should be no adverse record of you in the Hong Kong SAR; and second you should at least have visited Hong Kong SAR by air through the Hong Kong International Airport for more than 3 times in a year prior to the frequent visitor e-channel enrollment.

Once you successfully acquire this pass, you now use the Frequent Visitor e-Channels at the following airports:

- Hong Kong International Airport
- Macau Ferry Terminal
- Hung Hom
- Shenzhen Bay
- Sha Tau Kok
- Man Kam To

Chapter Two: Travel Essentials

- China Ferry Terminal
- Lo Wu
- Lok Ma Chau Spur Line
- Kai Tak Cruise Terminal
- Lok Ma Chau
- Tuen Mun Ferry Terminal

Traveller's Info

In this section, you will be provided with essential traveler's information on what to do and what not to do in Hong Kong. Be sure to keep all these essentials in mind while you are traveling.

Money Exchange, ATMs, Checks and Credit Cards

You may want to exchange your national money to a Hong Kong dollar at any authorized money changer. You should look for a Quality Tourism Services (QTS) Scheme to make sure that the money changer is accredited and safe.

You also have the option of exchanging your money at currency exchange counters located inside the Hong Kong International Airport. It is open from morning until night.

ATMs are found almost everywhere and are available 24/7. You can use international cards and also withdraw to various HSBC 'Electronic Money' machine, especially for MasterCard and Visa holders.

Chapter Two: Travel Essentials

Credit cards such as Visa, American Express, MasterCard, and Diners Club are accepted in various hotels, restaurants, and shops. You can easily tell what credit cards are accepted in a particular place by checking out their displayed sticker.

Traveler's checks encashment can be done through leading banks and also hotels. Be sure to inquire first to know the necessary requirements such as IDs or travel documents.

Electricity and Voltage

Hong Kong's standard electrical voltage is 220 volts AC, 50 Hz and majority of the outlets is a three-pronged style plug like in the UK. You may need a transformer to aid your electrical equipment or appliances. There are a lot of inexpensive adaptors that are sold at convenience and electrical/gadget stores.

Public Holidays

The only time that major shops and dining places or tourist attractions are close is usually during the first few days of the Chinese New Year. Most of them reopen for business on the third day; however, some convenience stores or local restaurants may stay closed for more than two days. If you want to know the public holidays of Hong Kong, you get updates online; it's also recommended that you call the shop or restaurant if you're not sure about their schedule of reopening during public holidays.

Health and Safety

Automatic sensors will measure your body temperature as soon as you arrived at the Hong Kong International Airport. If authorities think it's higher than average, you may be required to have a quick health check. You don't necessarily need vaccination certificates or other medical certificates, although it's better to check if your airline requires it.

- **Potable Water**

The tap water in Hong Kong is approved by the World Health Organization and therefore safe to drink. Mineral waters, including imported brands, can be found in stores and supermarkets.

- **Hospitals**

Hospitals in Hong Kong are readily available in case of any emergencies or accidents. The standard fee for medical attendance is $990; patients will always be treated even if they cannot pay immediately. Most medical professionals in public and private sectors can speak fluently in English.

- **Smoking restrictions**

Smokers are not welcome in Hong Kong. The city is implementing a smoking ban both for indoors and outdoors in all public transportations and carriers, hotels, malls, restaurants, beaches, school premises, supermarket, parks, etc. If you got caught smoking or carrying a lighter or unlighted cigarette or any kind of pipe in a non-smoking area you will pay $1,500 (Hong Kong dollars).

Safety Tips

- Do not leave your valuables unattended. Your money, passport or travel documents should be in a safe place, or you should carry it with you at all times.

- Be vigilant and watch out for your valuables especially in crowded places.

- Beware of people offering gambling opportunities or making attempts to distract you and steal your belongings.

Chapter Two: Travel Essentials

- Observe the rules and regulations of public places especially inside shopping malls and tourist spots

For your peace of mind, Hong Kong is frequently patrolled by police officers and they are very helpful, nonetheless, you still need to stay alerted and mindful at all times.

Public Hygiene and Environmental Regulations

Here are some rules you need to follow while wandering around Hong Kong.

- Do not eat or drink in public transportations.

- If you are caught littering, spitting or urinating in public venues, you will be fined with HK$1,500

- Public washrooms are clean and sanitary. Follow the rules inside public toilets

- Maintain cleanliness and clean as you go.

Chapter Two: Travel Essentials

Customs

Upon arriving at the airport in Hong Kong, you will need to be cleared by the department of customs. You must declare commodities and duty-free quotas. Here are some things to keep in mind:

- Importation and exportation of prohibited items such as dangerous drugs, firearms, weapons, plants, endangered species, and poultry must be accompanied by valid license, permit or certification issued in advance by relevant authorities unless exempted by law

- 'Mace Spray,' stun gun, tasers and other various personal protection devices, are also prohibited in Hong Kong.

- Do not include sharp objects such as blades, cutters or knives in your carry-on luggage. Pack these items in your check – in luggage.

- Do not carry liquid substances such as gels, aerosols, perfumes, etc. that are bigger than 100ml. For these items, place it in a single transparent and re-sealable bag, only one bag per passenger is allowed.

Chapter Two: Travel Essentials

Travel Insurance

It is highly recommended that you acquire travel insurance before traveling to Hong Kong. Inquire with your travel insurance company about the emergency coverage, contact numbers, and persons as well as the insurance policy. If you already have one, always carry with you the insurance policy and the insurance company hotline number for identification purposes in cases of emergencies.

Communication Services

Another central necessity that you need to have access to is the transmission lines and services. Obviously, when you get to another country, the mobile services, as well as internet services, will be different. Here are some things you need to keep in mind for you to be able to communicate effectively while in Hong Kong.

- **Hong Kong Tourist Sim Card**

This is one of the major things you need to buy as soon as you touch down in the city. The Hong Kong Tourist Sim card is created for tourists and travelers who will only stay for a few days or weeks. The sim card doesn't have or require subscription fees or other mobile charges. It is plug and text on the go!

Chapter Two: Travel Essentials

You can choose between a 5-day pass (HK$90) and 8-day pass (HK$120) tourist sim card. It comes with mobile data for you to have online access that can also have coverage in Mainland China, Macau and Taiwan. Of course, you can have unlimited calls and texts locally and internationally (although there will some extra mobile charges depending on the country).

You can buy the Hong Tourist Sim cards right at the Hong Kong International Airport and other convenience stores.

- **Wi-Fi Services**

These days we can't live anymore without being connected to the internet, especially when you're having fun in other places!

No worries, Hong Kong got you covered. There are many hotspots in the city particularly in the primary public locations and tourist destinations such as department stores, theme parks, gardens, centers, restaurants and dining places, hotels, transportation terminals, government buildings and public venues. All you have to do is to open your Wi-Fi and connect to 'CSL' SSID so that you can have free internet access. It also helps if you download the Wi-Fi HK App so that you have an idea on the location of hotspots in various places.

Chapter Two: Travel Essentials

Visitor Information Centers and Services

If in case you ran into a problem while in Hong Kong or would want to know about certain things and information, you can drop by at various Visitor Information Centers located around the major parts of the city including the Hong Kong International Airport (Lantau Island), the Peak (Hong Kong Island), Kowloon Peninsula and in Lo Wu.

Seasons in Hong Kong

Now that you have accomplished everything you need and perhaps learned and prepared for the necessary traveling essentials, the only thing left to do it to set out an itinerary right? Well, not yet! There is still one major factor you need to consider – the climate. You don't want to go against Mother Nature so to speak, and you don't want to also ruin your trip by not being prepared regarding the weather.

In this section, you will learn what to expect in Hong Kong's changing seasons so you can plan your trip accordingly.

Chapter Two: Travel Essentials

Climate and Weather

The city of Hong Kong has a sub-tropical climate; the only possible event that can ruin your trip or postponed it is typhoons. Fortunately, storms are very predictable - thanks to weather channels and modern technologies.
Usually, typhoons in Hong Kong begin in the month of May until November. Of course, when there is one approaching the city, the government announces it on different media channels, which is why you should check the weather first before setting a date for your trip or booking a ticket.

There will be warning signals to alert the locals as well as international transportations that will be announced by the Hong Kong Observatory, and there is also a separate warning system for torrential rains.

You might want to be guided by the Hong Kong Weather Information for Tourists website through this link: <http://visithk.weather.gov.hk/index_e.htm> for updates in weather conditions throughout the week, so you can be prepared.

Chapter Two: Travel Essentials

Seasons

Below is a brief overview of the seasons you can get to experience while in Hong Kong.

Spring (March to May)

Expect the dropping of temperature and humidity. Evenings can be cool. The average temperature during spring is 17oC – 26oC.

Summer (June to August)

Expect a hot and sunny temperature exceeding 31°C with high humidity levels. There are also occasional thunderstorms. Average Temperature during summer is 26oC – 31oC.

Autumn (September to November)

For tourists, this is the best time to visit Hong Kong; the temperature is comfortable, there's plenty of the sunshine and a great breeze around the city. Average Temperature during autumn is 19oC – 28oC.

Winter (December to February)

Expect a cool, cloudy and cold temperature. It can drop below 10°C in urban areas. The average temperature during winter is 12oC – 20oC.

Chapter Three: Getting In and Around Hong Kong

After learning the different requirements you need before traveling to this beautiful city, the next thing you should know is how to navigate around it. If you have enough knowledge regarding Hong Kong's port of entry and transportation services, you will quickly get to your destination with ease. So don't waste your time, energy and money, they are precious, and they should only be consumed by the spirit of Hong Kong. Learning how to navigate Hong Kong is the key to finding great places, meeting amazing people and saving a lot of money and time for a unique and one-of-a-kind experience.

Chapter Three: Getting In and Around In Hong Kong

In this chapter, you will learn the major transportation systems and port of entries as well as communication services to help you reach and explore different tourist destinations as well as, far-flung places. So grab your map and look out on the horizon, Hong Kong is waiting for you!

Traveling by Plane

The main gateway to Hong Kong is the award – winning Hong Kong International Airport that is operational 24 – hours a day. The city is an aviation hub wherein 100 plus airlines are connected to key towns and airports around the world.

How to Get to and from the Airport

Being one of the best airports in the world, the Hong Kong International Airport offers passengers and tourists a wide variety of transportation services and facilities to aid travelers into entering and leaving the city.

When you arrive in Hong Kong via an airline, you will have direct access to the following:

- Trains
- Buses/Shuttle Buses
- Taxis
- Ferries (if you choose to go to Mainland China)
- Hotel Transport Services

Chapter Three: Getting In and Around In Hong Kong

Traveling by Train

The Mass Transit Railway (MTR) is a high-speed transportation link from the airport to the city. It is the fastest and most efficient public transportation you can use to get to and from the airport. It will only take less than 35 minutes before you reach the island of Hong Kong from the airport. Hong Kong's MTR system will get you to larger districts around the city, and it also operates in mainland China through an inter-city train service.

MTR has 11 rail line including the Airport Express, Tsuen Wan, Island, South Island, Tung Chung, Kwun Tong, Tseung Kwan O, West Rail, East Rail, Ma On Shan, and Disneyland Resort. It also operates in the New Territories (Yuen Long and Tuen Mun)

Ticket Prices for Tourist Day Pass:
- Adult: $65
- Child: $30

Please note that the tourist day pass is unlimited (24 consecutive hours beginning from the first recorded entry) but it is only valid for one month from the date of issue. This pass is only available for visitors that are not Hong Kong residents. There are certain luggage exceptions that you need to be reminded of before getting on the train. For further information regarding these restricted valuables, please check their website.

Chapter Three: Getting In and Around In Hong Kong

Traveling by Buses

As soon as you arrive at the airport, turn right from the Arrival's Hall so that you can find several city buses and Airbuses that could take you around the island. There are different buses available in Hong Kong such as minibusses, routes buses and double-deckers that are accessible for tourists so that you can have a view of the city during your ride. These buses are safe, comfortable and mostly air-conditioned.

You can take 'A' routes airbuses; there are about 12 of them, these buses can bring you to major locations in the city, as well as the Kowloon Peninsula and the New Territories such as Lantau Island.
Almost all bus lines cover routes in and around the city. Make sure to check first the final destinations that are displayed at the front of the bus before getting in; the signs are bilingual.

Here are the bus lines that you can take to and from the airport:
- Kowloon Motor Bus
- New World First Bus
- New Lantao Bus (usually runs around Lantau Island)
- Long Win Bus (mainly operates in North Lantau Island)

Chapter Three: Getting In and Around In Hong Kong

Minibuses

If you prefer direct access to specific places in Hong Kong, you can take the green minibuses that are also around the airport. These buses can only carry 16 passengers, and it has a fixed price for specific routes.

You can also ride red minibuses but these coaches don't follow a fixed route, and it will not stop for a new passenger along the road unless there is an available seat. You can get off along the routes unless it is prohibited. You should have an exact fare if you are going to pay in cash; they are also accepting Octopus cards (more on this later).

Fares for Buses:

All of the bus lines require an exact amount or an exact change if you pay in cash. They are accepting Octopus cards as well. The price for the bus ride is based on the distance traveled.

Traveling by Taxi

Just like buses, taxis or cabs are always available in the pick-up area of the airport. These taxis can also be hailed in the streets or contacted by phone for service. They are all metered, air-conditioned, fairly inexpensive and clean. The information regarding charges is often displayed inside the vehicle.

Chapter Three: Getting In and Around In Hong Kong

The taxis in Hong Kong are categorized by three colors. You will be given an overview below regarding the designated routes/geographical area for the color coded taxis as well as its corresponding average fares.

- **Red Taxis**

These taxis are the primary transport system throughout Hong Kong's island with a few exceptions such as the Tung Chung Road on Lantau Island and the entire south side of Lantau Island.
Fare: Starts at HK$22.00

- **Green Taxis**

The routes of these taxis are only applicable if you want to get to the New Territories or nearby islands that are not within Hong Kong.
Fare: Starts at HK$18.50

- **Blue Taxis**

These taxis are only for passengers that are heading to the Lantau Island. It is only exclusive for this trip.
Fare: Starts at HK$17

Chapter Three: Getting In and Around In Hong Kong

Taxi Service

There are also accessible taxi services for senior citizens, passengers with a disability as well as travelers with bulky or heavy luggage. These taxis can be requested through a phone. Here are some of the recommended taxi services you can avail:

- **Diamond Cab**

This taxi can only accommodate a maximum of two wheelchair users on a single trip. Only two to five passengers (caretakers/relatives) without wheelchairs are allowed.

- **SynCab**

This taxi can only accommodate a maximum of one wheelchair user on a single trip. Only two to four passengers (caretakers/relatives) without wheelchairs are allowed.

If you have any complaints regarding the taxis, you can call the Transport Complaints Unit hotline at +852 2889 9999. For lost properties on the taxis, you can call +852 1872 920.

Chapter Three: Getting In and Around In Hong Kong

Traveling by Ferry

From the Hong Kong International Airport, you can explore the city through the different ferry ports in the Pearl River Delta; the good thing is that you don't need to go through immigration and customs since you have already gone through airport security.

Ferries in Hong Kong Island are regularly operational. Its routes from the city are connected in the Kowloon Peninsula as well as outlying islands such as the Peng Chau, Discovery Bay, Cheung Chau, Lamma Island as well as Lantau Island. You can choose for a regular ferry or opt in for fast boats, but of course, it can be quite expensive. Here is the list of the different ferry companies you may want to try in Hong Kong:

- **New World First Ferry Services Ltd**

Services: Cheung Chau, Lantau Island, and Peng Chau

Tel: +852 2131 8181

Website: www.nwff.com.hk

- **The Hong Kong & Kowloon Ferry Ltd**

Services: Lamma Island and Peng Chau

Tel: +852 2815 6063

Website: www.hkkf.com.hk

Chapter Three: Getting In and Around In Hong Kong

- **Discovery Bay Transportation Services Ltd**

Services: Discovery Bay, Lantau Island

Tel: +852 3651 2345

Website: www.visitdiscoverybay.com

- **Park Island Transport Company Limited**

Services: Ma Wan Island

Tel: +852 2946 8888

Website: www.pitcl.com.hk

Traveling by Trams

If you want to explore the ins and outs of the city in a fun way particularly on the north corridor of Hong Kong, you can use one of the oldest and most affordable transportation – trams. These historical trams had been around since 1904, they are double-decker streetcars much like a train, and it's a unique way to view the area.

If you travel through trams, the most common route and district that you are going to pass through are Wan Chai, Happy Valley, Causeway Bay and North Point. Trams such as the Peak Tram usually open from 7 am until midnight. Other trams operate very early in the morning with a 15-minute interval.

The Peak Tram

Fare: $2.30 (flat rate)

Chapter Three: Getting In and Around In Hong Kong

It is required that you pay an exact amount or exact change if you are paying in cash. Octopus cards are also accepted.

Octopus Cards

Octopus Cards functions as a stored-value e-card that is mainly used to pay for transportations such as MTR, trams, buses or taxis. Locals also use this card when purchasing goods in supermarket, malls, convenience stores, fast food, restaurants, vending machines and the like. It is extremely versatile and handy, especially for tourists. This can give you access to the necessities you need when touring around Hong Kong. By using the Octopus card, you won't have to worry about always finding money changers to exchange your foreign cash to Hong Kong dollars.

There are many types of Octopus Cards, one of which is the Sold Tourist Octopus card which is made for tourists and short time travelers. The cost of this is around HK$39 (prices may change over time). The Sold Tourist Octopus card can be brought in as a souvenir because it has a cool Hong Kong design printed on it. The great thing about this is you can still use it when you come back to the city. Just make sure that it does not tamper, or the card is still readable.

Chapter Three: Getting In and Around In Hong Kong

Another type is an On-Loan Octopus card which has a refundable deposit of HK$50, but it is only valid for about 90 days.

Chapter Three: Getting In and Around In Hong Kong

Chapter Four: Hotels and Accommodations

After learning about the ports of entry in Hong Kong and the different ways on how you can get around this beautiful city, the next thing you should know after arriving at the airport is where to stay. There are tons of options online and a lot of feedback from friends, and family who have stayed in the city - not to mention the thousands of social reviews and comments on different social networking sites.

Chapter Four: Hotels and Accommodations

The million dollar question is - where should you stay and how in the world are you going to choose the best accommodation in this dynamic city?

In this chapter you will be provided with the list of what we consider to be the top 10 best hotel districts in Hong Kong. Some are very expensive, while others are a bit more cost-friendly. The variety of hotel accommodations you can probably expect may include any of the following:

- Hostels
- Bed & Breakfast
- Budget Hotels (2-3 star ratings)
- 4 Star Hotels
- 5 Star Hotels
- Apartments for short-term lease
- Rooms for rent
- Family Rooms for rent

If you want to know the best fit for you in every aspect – financial, proximity, ambiance and overall experience, check out the following recommended hotel areas or accommodation district below.

Chapter Four: Hotels and Accommodations

1. Central (Hong Kong Island)

This is the central business district of the city, hence the name. It is one of the earliest developed areas in Hong Kong Island, and it is also considered as the financial hub of the city. It is located on the North Shore of Hong Kong and can be easily reached by buses, airport express, taxis and MTR (Central Station) in less than 30 minutes.

You can find a lot of multinational corporations such as banks and financial companies. There are a lot of businesses around the area, as well as several consulate embassies; it is also where the Government Hill (Hong Kong's government headquarters) can be found, which means that the price for

Chapter Four: Hotels and Accommodations

staying in this district is very high compare to other parts of the city. In fact, this is the second most expensive place to stay in Hong Kong. Businessmen, politicians, government officials, entrepreneurs and tourists from all over the world are usually the people staying in this area. You can expect to see a lot of 5-star hotels and accommodations with the most luxurious facilities as well as high-end boutiques. So if the expense is not a problem, this is one of the most recommended places you should stay in.

The sights nearby this district are Sky Terrace 428, Peak Galleria, Peak Tower, Madame Tussauds Wax Museum, Zoological and Botanical Garden, St. John's Cathedral, Statue Square, Dr. Sun Yatsen Museum, The Flagstaff House Museum of Tea Ware as well as the state-of-the-art skyscrapers and buildings of HSBC, IFC, Bank of America and Bank of China who participates in the Symphony of Lights every day at around 8pm. Here's a quick overview of the famous hotels as well as cheap accommodations around the Central district of Hong Kong:

- Four Seasons
- Conrad
- JW Marriott
- Landmark Mandarin Oriental
- Shangri-La Hotel
- The Upper Central
- Ovolo Central

Chapter Four: Hotels and Accommodations

- The Pottinger Hong Kong
- Hotel LKF
- Shama Central Service Apartment

2. *Wan Chai*

Wan Chai formerly called Ha Wan, is the home for Hong Kong's most important fairs and events gathering such as conventions, exhibition centre, concerts, expos, festivals etc. Similar to Central, Wan Chai is also one of the oldest districts in the city. This area is also famous for its nightlife because it is filled with different kinds of bars, upscale nightclubs, pubs and restaurants. You can also find high-end shopping centers and fine dining. It is mainly an

Chapter Four: Hotels and Accommodations

entertainment and business district which can be both perfect for businessmen and tourists who wanted to relax after holding important meetings in the city.

Wan Chai can be reached by buses, MTR (Island Line station), taxis, and Star Ferry. The sights and events you can expect to see are the Hong Kong Convention and Exhibition Centre in the Golden Bauhinia Square, Goethe Gallery, Hong Kong Academy for Performing Arts, Happy Valley, Wan Chai Computer City, Wooloomooloo Bar, Habitat Lounge, Plateau Spa, Happy Foot, Sun Street bars and café etc.

Here's a quick overview of the famous hotels as well as cheap accommodations around the Wan Chai district of Hong Kong:

- Grand Hyatt Hotel
- Dorsett Wanchai
- Butterfly on Morrison
- Renaissance Hong Kong Harbour View Hotel
- Kew Green Hotel Wanchai
- Hotel Indigo
- Ozo Wesley
- Cosmopolitan Hotel
- Gloucester Luk Kwok
- Metropark Hotel Wan Chai

Chapter Four: Hotels and Accommodations

3. *Tsim Sha Tsui (TST)*

The locals refer to this place only as TST; it is located in the Kowloon Peninsula and because of its location, it is truly the place where east meets west. This part of Hong Kong is the major tourist spot because there are a lot of destinations you can explore. It is also the hub of major transportations like the MTR (there are 3 MTR lines around Kowloon) and the famous Star Ferry.

The popular Nathan Road also begins and ends (depending on your perspective) in the peninsula. Just like Central and Wan Chai, TST offers a lot of shopping and dining places as well as unique bars and café. The best part

Chapter Four: Hotels and Accommodations

about this place is that it is walking distance to the iconic Victoria Harbour.

The major attractions you can go to while staying in TST are the Victoria Harbour, Avenue of Stars (such as Bruce Lee statue), Hong Kong Museum of Art, Clock Tower, Hong Kong Science Musem, Hong Kong Cultural Center, Chungking Mansion, Kowloon Park, Harbour City, Charlie Brown Café, Sky100 Observation Deck (Western Kowloon) and Ozone Bar (one of the highest bar in the world).

Here's a quick overview of the famous hotels around the Tsim Sha Tsui district of Hong Kong:

- The Peninsula
- InterContinental
- Hullet House
- Sheraton
- Hyatt Hotel
- Marco Polo Hotel
- Hotel Skylark
- The Mira Hong Kong
- Holiday Inn Golden Mile
- Butterfly on Prat Boutique Hotel

4. Causeway Bay

Causeway Bay is the most expensive area to stay in, in all of Hong Kong, but it's definitely a must-see and must comeback place for tourists. A lot of first time tourists say that once you go in this place, it's like you have captured the heart of Hong Kong. Lots of people keep coming back in this town for tons of reasons – the shops, the food, the entertainment, the attractions, the museums, the art, the festivals, the historic landmarks and the people. This is the equivalent of Times Square in New York.

Chapter Four: Hotels and Accommodations

Causeway Bay is most famous for its iconic shops and extravagant lifestyle. Even if you are not a shopaholic type, after experiencing this place, you will be! Not only is this town packed with the grandest boutiques and stores, it is also dense with the coolest and hippest people. It's the fashion centre of Hong Kong. This is a shopping paradise that shoppers dream of. Some malls and streets you can check out are the Fashion Walk, Jardine's Crescent, World Trade Center, Hysan Place (up to 17 floors of shopping area) – set to become Causeway Bay's major shopping landmark.

If you don't like shopping but would want to see other interesting places, Causeway Bay also offers numerous fine dining, bars, restaurants as well as lots of historic places and famous roads you can visit and take a picture of such as Victoria Park, Noonday Gun (northeast of Causeway Bay), Hong Kong Central Library etc. It can be reached through riding the MTR (Causeway Bay station), ferry, buses, taxis and you can also ride on trams to get around the area.

Expect to spend lots of money – by lots, I mean thousands of HK dollars, especially in accommodations if you choose to stay in Causeway Bay.

Here's a quick overview of the famous hotels around the Causeway Bay district of Hong Kong:

- The Excelsior
- Crowne Plaza

Chapter Four: Hotels and Accommodations

- Best Western
- Metropark Causeway Bay
- Regal Empire Hotel
- Lanson Place
- Charterhouse Causeway Bay
- J Plus Boutique Hotel
- Galaxy Hotel Causeway Bay
- Gloucester Hotel

5. Mong Kok

Similar to Causeway Bay, Mong Kok is one of the most populated areas of Hong Kong. The English translation of Mong Kok is "bustling corner."

Chapter Four: Hotels and Accommodations

The only main difference between Causeway Bay and Mong Kok is that Mong Kok is made up of street markets than luxurious malls or department stores. This is where merchants sell the same product in one whole street, so if you love shopping but don't have that much money to spend, you can go in Mong Kok and exercise your bargaining power!

Lots of competition means that you can get certain products next to nothing. This place is also a hub of large food stalls that are inexpensive. You should check out the Ladies Market, Electronic Street, Sneaker Street, Bird Garden, Flower Market, Jade Market, SaSa, Grand Century Place and the famous Wong Tai Sin Temple. Hotels in Mong Kok are a lot cheaper and are near main establishments and transportations.

Here's a quick overview of the famous hotels around the Causeway Bay district of Hong Kong:

- Cordis Hotel
- Royal Plaza Hotel
- Holiday Inn Express Hotel
- Ming Du Hotel
- Sunny Day Hotel
- Lodgewood by L'Hotel
- Silka West Hotel
- Rosedale Hotel

Chapter Four: Hotels and Accommodations

- Langham Place Mong Kok
- Oriental Lander Hotel

6. *Sheung Wan*

Sheung Wan is also called the upper district or the gateway district mainly because this is where the British forces entered before occupying the whole island of Hong Kong. Sheung Wan is located in the northern west area of Hong Kong and it is where ancient street life meets the sleek corporate world.

If you want to go around this "very chinese" part of Hong Kong, you can ride the famous Ding Ding tram.

Chapter Four: Hotels and Accommodations

It is also best to explore Sheung Wan by foot so that you can connect more with the locals. The Western Market, Hollywood Road, Cat Street, Man Mo Temple, Mid-level escalator and Seafood Street are among the cool places you should check out.

Hotels and accommodations in Sheung Wan is much more affordable for tourists, here's a quick overview of hotels you could stay in around the area:

- Ovolo Noho
- Hotel LBP
- iClub Sheung Wan Hotel
- Butterfly on Hollywood
- 99 Bonham All Suite Hotel
- Ibis Hotel Sheung Wan
- ECO Tree Hotel
- The Mercer Boutique
- Holiday Inn Express Sheung Wan
- CHI Residences 138

Chapter Four: Hotels and Accommodations

7. Lantau Island

If you choose to stay away from all the hustle and bustle of the Hong Kong Island, you can go to one of the outlying islands or the New Territories of Hong Kong, one of which is the Lantau Island. The great advantage of choosing to stay in this district is the tons of cheap but quality hotels and accommodations that surround it as well as the historical places you can explore. The island can be reached easily and quickly by taking the MTR, or you could also choose to have a ferry ride. Buses and taxis are also means of transportation to get around this great area.

Chapter Four: Hotels and Accommodations

One of the highlights of Lantau Island is the Ngong Ping Plateau wherein you will have to ride the Ngong Ping cable car to get there. There are also lots of other attractions such as the Big Buddha, Tai O fishing village, Po Lin Monastery and the Hong Kong Disneyland.

There are lots of 5 star hotels in Lantau Island as well as inexpensive accommodations for tourists, here's a quick overview of hotels you could stay in around the area:

- Novotel City Gate
- Hong Kong SkyCity Marriott Hotel
- Tai O Heritage Hotel
- Hong Kong Disneyland Hotel
- Disney's Hollywood Hotel
- Auberge Discovery Bay

Chapter Four: Hotels and Accommodations

8. *Peng Chau Island*

For tourists who wanted to really zone out and just relax, Peng Chau Island is the district for you. It is one of the outlying islands in Hong Kong that tourists can explore if they love beaches and resorts. The best part about Peng Chau is that, not only are the hotels cheap but also its fine dining, there's a bounty of seafood restaurants to choose from, and uncharted territories to explore which is best suited for outdoors person.

This place is not yet fully developed and that is precisely why lots of tourists want to stay here, the nature and scenery

Chapter Four: Hotels and Accommodations

is breathtaking and very far away from the fast-pace lifestyle of that in the Hong Kong Island. Aside from the beaches and resorts, some places you could explore are Tin Hau temple, Golden Flower Shrine, Finger Hill and the Peng Chau Heritage Trail.

Here's a quick overview of the famous hotels near the Peng Chau district of Hong Kong:

- Le Meridien Cyberport
- Hotel Jen
- Ramada Hotel

Chapter Four: Hotels and Accommodations

9. *Lamma Island*

Lamma Island is also one of the outlying islands outside the city of Hong Kong. This area is perfect for people who are into hiking or trekking. There are also resorts and crystal clear beaches as well as seafood restaurants. The fishery customs and traditions in this place is also one of the things first time tourists' needs to experience.

Hotels and accommodations in this area are also inexpensive, and this town is also accessible to major transportations especially the ferries. Some places you could visit are the main town which is called Yung Shue Wan and also Sok Kwu Wan (the fishing village).

Chapter Four: Hotels and Accommodations

Here's a quick overview of the famous hotels near the Lamma Island district of Hong Kong:

- Concerto Inn
- Bali Holiday Resort
- Dollarful
- Sun Hing Hotel

10. Stanley Village

The last but definitely not the least is Stanley. It is located in the southern part of Hong Kong facing the South China Sea and is only 45 minutes away from the Central by bus. The small town of Stanley maintains its characteristic as

Chapter Four: Hotels and Accommodations

being a quaint village wherein you can shop for goods such as ornaments, jewelries and clothing as well as Chinese souvenirs that you could buy for your friends and family. It is both a hit with locals and tourists when it comes to shopping for items because the alleys are not crowded and it is so relaxing unlike in main parts of the city.

Getting to Stanley is the best part; you will surely enjoy the ride because of the scenery, the bays and beaches nearby especially the amazing view of the South China Sea. There are also lots of seafood restaurants and cheap food stalls you can find. One of the main attractions in Stanley aside from the Stanley Market and the resorts, is the Murray House, so be sure to make that one of your stops. You can find lots of hotels nearby and several accommodations that can be inexpensive.

Here's a quick overview of the famous hotels near the Stanley Village district of Hong Kong:

- Stanley Oriental Hotel
- MiniHotel
- L'hotel Island South
- Caritas Oswald Cheung International House
- The Emperor Hotel Happy Valley

Chapter Four: Hotels and Accommodations

Chapter Five: Shop and Dine

Once you have decided what district you're going to stay in for your trip, the next thing you should know is the places where you could eat and shop at the same time.

The great thing about Hong Kong's districts is that the malls' and restaurants' proximity are very convenient and accessible. It's perfect for tourists who love to spend the whole day buying goodies and then eating afterwards.

There are several shopping alleys and lots of food places to choose from. In this chapter, we've put together the

Chapter Five: Shop and Dine

list of the top 10 shopping and dining districts in and around Hong Kong that you should not dare miss!

These are the places where shopaholics meet the food fanatics! Brace yourself; gluttony is at its best.

1. *Tang Lung Street*

Tang Lung Street is located in Causeway Bay Hong Kong. There are lots of shopping malls and department stores in the main street alongside with tons of variety of food stalls and restaurants you could choose from. Tang Lung is famous for its cheap snacks and delicious gourmet food that you could grab while wandering around its busy

Chapter Five: Shop and Dine

street. There are also lots of tea houses, Japanese restaurants and Western bars that are open until nighttime.

Here's a quick overview of the restaurants and food stalls you need to check out while in Tang Lung:

- Koheitsu
- Rakuen
- Shirokiya
- Ajitomi
- I-mode
- Seorae
- Sushi Mori
- The Drunken Pot
- Ootoya
- Wang Jia Sha
- Dong Lai Shun
- Kamameshi

Chapter Five: Shop and Dine

2. *Nga Tsin Wai Road*

Nga Tsin Wai road is located in the gourmet capital of Hong Kong which is the Kowloon Peninsula.

This street in particular is the hub of all Asian delicacies; Chinese and Thai restaurants dominate the place alongside several stores and malls. The food stalls and dining places are quite inexpensive; there are also lots of other international cuisines you could choose from.

Here's a quick overview of the restaurants and food stalls you need to check out while in Nga Tsin Wai Road:

- Noah Castella
- Lucky Food
- Lok Yuen

Chapter Five: Shop and Dine

- Watanabe-Ya
- Tso Choi Restaurant
- Hoover Cake Shop
- Seasons Patisserie
- Tso Choi Restaurant
- Ma Chai
- Mrs. Sweetie

3. Nathan Road

Nathan Road is known for having one of the largest international choices of food in Hong Kong. Aside from delicious Asian gourmet, you can also find tons of western restaurants and international cuisines particularly African and Indian cuisines. You can expect a lot of curry dishes in this road as well as coffee shops. The costs of some of these high-end restaurants are quite expensive, but there are also other food and dining places around the area that are much more affordable. Nathan Road is very accessible for tourists and commuters; it is located in Tsim Sha Tsui and also surrounded by malls, shopping alleys and fashion boutiques.

Here's a quick overview of the restaurants and food stalls you need to check out while in Prince Edward Road:

- Running Chicken
- MeokBang Korean BBQ & Bar
- Madam's Kitchen
- Prince Dragon
- The Alchemist Café Bistro
- Dazzling Café
- Hiroshi
- Cambo
- Harlan's
- Mekiki no Ginji

Chapter Five: Shop and Dine

4. Lan Kwai Fong

About twenty years ago, the area of Lan Kwai Fong was quite unpopular and not prosperous, but today this area became one of the most sought after shopping and dining destinations for tourists as well as locals together with SoHo Hollywood. You can also eat your heart out in Lan Kwai Fong's western restaurants. There are lots of Mexican, Italian, French and American cuisines to choose from.

Chapter Five: Shop and Dine

You can find 3 major streets in Lan Kwai Fong that is known for its ambience these are the Elgin Street, Shelley Steet, and Staunton Street.

Here's a quick overview of the restaurants and food stalls you need to check out while in Lan Kwai Fong:

- Casa Lisboa
- Portuguese Resta & Bar
- Gold by Harlan Goldstein
- Fofo by el Willy
- Brickhouse
- Souvla
- Insomnia
- Lily & Bloom
- Mesa
- Bistecca Italian Steak House

Chapter Five: Shop and Dine

5. Canton Road

Canton Road is located in Tsim Sha Tsui, Hong Kong. This road is known for a mixture of Western, European and Asian cuisines. There are lots of hotpots and bars as well as British pubs that last until midnight. It is near many shopping districts and restaurants have a variety of local and international gourmet.

Here's a quick overview of the restaurants and food stalls you need to check out while in Canton Road:

- Sushi Hiro
- Tonkichi Tonkatsu Seafood
- Wa-En Yakiniku
- Sushi Dokoro Matsudo

Chapter Five: Shop and Dine

- Zenpachi Shabu Shabu
- Yakichi
- The Sweet Dynasty
- Ran Sushi
- Hsin Kuang Seafood Restaurant
- Manakamana Nepali Restaurant

6. Hung Hom

If you want to savor the eastern cuisines, Hung Hom is te place to go. This place is a relatively new gourmet dist5ict that is very accessible and also convenient after buying goodies from different stores surrounding it. It specializes in home made cooking and unique Asian taste. The Whampoa

Chapter Five: Shop and Dine

Gourmet Place is the most popular dining place in Hung Hom, you can find more than 10 restaurants and food stalls that offer the best of Chinese, Vietnamese, Singaporean and Filipino dishes.

Here's a quick overview of the restaurants and food stalls you need to check out while in Hung Hom:

- Tenno Ramen
- Si Sun Fast Food
- Steam Fresh
- Promenade Restaurant
- Mikawaya
- Café Charm's
- King's Dynasty
- Yvonne's Noodle
- Spicy Girl
- Chili Party 2.0

Chapter Five: Shop and Dine

7. *Percival Street*

Percival Street is located in the culinary capital of Asia which is in Causeway Bay. The mouthwatering food and restaurants in this road is hard to resist. You can find tons of cheap and expensive restaurants as well as Japanese sushi bars and dai pai dong (Hong Kong style food service). Department stores are surrounding the area as well. Here's a quick overview of the restaurants and food stalls you need to check out while in Percival Street:

- Shabu Sen
- Bbim Monster
- Sweet Basil Thai Cuisine
- Sunning Restaurant

Chapter Five: Shop and Dine

- Paradise Dynasty
- Pacific Coffee Company
- Chee Kei
- Beidouweng Hotpot Cuisine
- Watami Japanese Casual Restaurant
- U-Banquet

8. *Lung Kong Road*

If you are fond of eating desserts and sweets, then Lung Kong Road should be one of your stops while you are in the Kowloon Peninsula. This is one of the traveller's choices if when it comes to buying Chinese or Asian delicacies.

Chapter Five: Shop and Dine

There are also several Chinese and Thai restaurants around the area. Kowloon's shopping district is also near the Lung Kong Road so if you need the energy to do more shopping, it's best to spend a few minutes to grab a bite in this popular street. Lung Kong Road is famous for the Lung Kong Restaurant and the Islam Food Restaurant.

9. *Stanley Road*

Stanley Road is famous for its Asian seafood restaurants with a touch of Western cuisine. If you want to escape the luxurious cities and food places in mainland Hong Kong, Stanley Road is worth a try. You can have a view of the South China Sea while eating fresh sea foods straight from

Chapter Five: Shop and Dine

the ocean! There are also a lot of bars that are open well into the night and its shopping alleys are not crowded which is a great thing if you want to leisurely buy traditional Chinese souvenirs and goodies while experiencing the breathtaking area.

Here's a quick overview of the restaurants and food stalls you need to check out while in Chatam Road:

- Wing's Kitchen
- Tai Fung Lau Peking Restaurant
- Madame Hanoi Vietnamese Restaurant
- King's Lodge
- One Little Room
- The Lucky House
- Retro Café
- The White Tower Restaurant
- Tony's Grill
- King Edward VII

Chapter Five: Shop and Dine

10. Sai Kung

If you love eating seafood while enjoying beautiful scenery without the hustle and bustle of the city, then Sai Kung is the place for you. There are several seafood restaurants and dining places around the area that you can buy for yourself in their seafood market. You can be sure of the quality and freshness of what you are going to eat because it is handpicked by you! It is a seaside style of eating that you can only find in Lamma Island - one of Hong Kong's outlying islands and part of the New Territories.

Chapter Five: Shop and Dine

Most restaurants have an open-air seating so that customers can fully taste and breathe the seaside experience.

Here's a quick overview of the restaurants and food stalls you need to check out while in Sai Kung:

- Let's Jam
- Sing Kee Seafood Restaurant
- Golden Chicken
- Loaf On
- Golden Chicken
- Ice Mango Café
- Chuen Kee Seafood Restaurant
- The Cabin Café & Restaurant
- AJ's Sri Lankan Cuisine
- Seafood Island Restaurant

Chapter Five: Shop and Dine

Chapter Six: Tourist Spots in Hong Kong

Aside from shopping and dining around this great city, the major thing that you need to check off your bucket list in this trip is to see and experience the famous and the most popular tourist destinations in Hong Kong. In this chapter, we have put together the list of the top 10 must see and must visit places in Hong Kong.

It doesn't matter if you're a history buff, a local, religious or someone who loves the outdoors. These ten places in its own way will amaze and inspire you; they will trace you back to its history and connect you to the future; and most importantly all of them will teach you to savor the moment. Carpe diem!

Chapter Six: Tourist Spots in Hong Kong

1. Victoria Peak

The Victoria Peak is also known as Mount Austin or simply The Peak. It stands at about 1,800 feet making it the highest mountain in Hong Kong. It is located in Central Hong Kong and as soon as you reached the top you'll be able to see the spectacular skyline the city has to offer.

First time travellers should not dare miss going to Victoria Peak otherwise you will miss Hong Kong's most iconic cite and most exclusive neighborhood since the colonial times. You can ride the historic Peak Tram while overlooking Hong Kong's major areas such as the Central, Victoria Harbour, Lamma Island and the outlying islands.

Chapter Six: Tourist Spots in Hong Kong

Getting to the top of the Victoria Peak while riding the Peak Tram is a great visual experience, however, the awesomeness doesn't stop there.

Once you are at the top of the mountain there are many things you can go and do. You can go to Sky Terrace 428 for a breath taking view of the city, you can check out the Peak Tower and the Peak Galleria where there is an observation deck that is free of charge, and if you want to just hang around and immerse yourself in this amazing landscape, you can tour around The Peak Circle Walk that stretches about 3.5 kilometers, don't worry though, there are lots of dining places and restaurants around the area as well as small shopping alleys you can stop by.

There are more than seven million visitors a year, and the Peak is also a residential area – thanks to Hong Kong's accessible transportations.

Here's how you can get to the iconic Victoria Peak; ride a bus 15C from Central Pier 8. You can also walk from MTR Central Station and exit at J2 for you to be able to take the Peak Tram from the Peak Tram Lower Terminus on Garden Road. Another option is take a bus ride in 15 from Exchange Square bus terminus which is near the MTR Hong Kong Station located in Exit D. You can also ride a minibus from the public transport interchange found in MTR Hong Kong Station (Exit E).

Chapter Six: Tourist Spots in Hong Kong

2. Hong Kong Disneyland

The influence of Mickey Mouse is indeed truly remarkable! America has brought its most iconic tourist destination to the east – the Hong Kong Disneyland.

The Hong Kong Disneyland theme park is located in Lantau Island particularly in Penny's Bay. It officially opened to Asian and international visitors on September 12 2005. The most interesting fact about the Hong Kong Disneyland is that the structure of it was aligned with a Chinese tradition which is Feng Shui.

For instance, there was a bend in the walkway near the theme park's resort entrance so that the qi energy will not flow into the South China Sea.

Chapter Six: Tourist Spots in Hong Kong

Just like in America, the Hong Kong Disneyland consists of seven major themed areas; these are Main Street, Adventureland, Fantasyland, Toy Story Land, Tommorrowland, Mystic Point, and Grizzly Gulch. The cast members speak multilingual language including English, Cantonese and Mandarin. The guide maps are also printed in different Asian languages such as Chinese, Japanese, Malay, Indonesian and Thai.

Since its opening in 2005, the Hong Kong Disneyland already catered to 25 million tourists all over the world with around 8 – 9 million visitors per annum.

The theme park has also different activities that adults or young-at-hearts can enjoy such as the Disney Haunted Halloween, Disney in the Stars which is a pyrotechnic show with spectacular fireworks at night in sync with classic songs, and Disney Paint in the Night Parade as well as Flights of Fantasy Parade. Families can also relax and have a good time staying at the Disneyland Resort and the Hollywood Hotel.

The Hong Kong Disneyland is very accessible and convenient; there is a direct MTR line from the Sunny Bay Station to the Disneyland Resort Station. You can also take the Disneyland Shuttle bus and even ride the Long Win Bus which operates 3 routes to Disneyland. If you are coming from Central Hong Kong, it will take about 40 minutes by train, and about 30 – 40 minutes if you are coming from Tsim Sha Tsui.

Chapter Six: Tourist Spots in Hong Kong

3. Hong Kong Ocean Park

If you can't get enough of Disneyland and its amazing theme park, why not try going to Hong Kong's very own Ocean Park? Let the wildness and serenity of the ocean inspire you!

The Hong Kong Ocean Park opened its doors to the public in 1977. During 1979 – 1997, Ocean Park was the most popular destination in Hong Kong because of its signature killer whale called Miss Hoi Wai. However, in 2005, its sales declined because of its rival theme park – Disneyland. Nevertheless, it still continued operating and had become

Chapter Six: Tourist Spots in Hong Kong

more profitable because lots of tourists also prefer going here.

The Ocean Park is known for its beautiful Oceanarium, marine mammal park, animal theme park as well as amusement park. It is located between Wong Chuk Hang and Nam Long Shan in Hong Kong's southern district.

The Ocean Park has an Ocean Express Railway which is a one-of-a-kind cable car system to reach the two areas that are separated by a mountain – the Summit (headland) and the Waterfront (Lowland). Visitors can also use the second largest escalator in Hong Kong to reach the Summit.

Aside from its flagship Oceanarium, there is also a theme park much like Disneyland. There are a variety of animal exhibits, rainforest and polar displays, giant panda habitat and one of the world's largest aquarium domes.

The Ocean Park's latest attraction is a 20,000 sq. ft. shark aquarium that was opened to the public in 2014.

If you want to go to the Ocean Park, you can take the MTR (Ocean Park Station) Exit B. Then you need to ride the City bus Route 629; this bus is operational daily from the MTR or Central Pier No. 7

Chapter Six: Tourist Spots in Hong Kong

4. Jumbo Kingdom (Aberdeen Harbour)

The Jumbo Kingdom which means Treasure Kingdom is composed of Jumbo Floating Restaurants. It is located in Aberdeen Harbour particularly in Aberdeen South Typhoon Shelter which is also one of Hong Kong's most famous tourist attractions. It was opened to the public in 1971. This place not just only offers great food but also great scenery.

It has been featured on numerous Hollywood films including Jackie Chan's Enter the Dragon.

Several notable personalities and celebrities have been to this place as well such as Queen Elizabeth II, David Bowie, Gwyneth Paltrow, and Tom Cruise. More than 30 million tourists visit the harbor and eat in the Jumbo Restaurant.

Chapter Six: Tourist Spots in Hong Kong

Getting to the Jumbo Kingdom can be quite tricky, but transportations are very convenient and accessible. If you want to go to this place, take the MTR (Wong Chuk Hang station) and go out in Exit B, and then transfer to a bus going to Aberdeen Terminal. Once you get there you need to walk about 5 – 10 minutes towards the Shum Wan Pier for a free ferry shuttle going to the restaurant.

5. Avenue of Stars

Similar to the Hollywood Walk of Fame in Los Angeles, the Avenue of Stars honors the celebrities and notable filmmakers of the Hong Kong Film Industry. It is located in Tsim Sha Tsui along the Victoria Harbour. This is where Bruce Lee's statue is erected; he is one of the legends in martial arts and most notable Chinese Hollywood personality. It was opened to the public in 2004, and millions of tourists drop by to take pictures of these famous celebrities. Just like in the Hollywood Walk of Fame, the names of Hong Kong's notable filmmakers and artists are also cemented on the road. If you want to go to these awesome place, just ride the MTR (East Tsim Sha Tsui Station) and Exit in J. It will take just about a few minutes from the InterContinental Hotel to the Avenue of Stars. Everything is walking distance from there.

6. Hong Kong Museum of History

If you are a history buff or someone who is just interested in Hong Kong's rich history and culture, then it is recommended that you go to the renowned Hong Kong

Chapter Six: Tourist Spots in Hong Kong

Museum of History. Tourists and even locals love to come to this place to learn about Hong Kong's heritage. It is located in Kowloon Peninsula in Tsim Sha Tsui and was founded in 1975. It is collection of the countless artifacts and objects that are part of China and Hong Kong's natural history, ethnography, archaeological, and local history. 400 years of history was compressed into one 7,000 square meter of space! Exhibitions are also held inside the museum from time to time.

    If you want to get to this place just take the MTR (Tsim Sha Tsui) station and Exit in B2, then walk for about 15 minutes along the Cameron Road towards East Tsim Sha Tsui. You can also get off at Jordan Station and Exit in D, then walk in the Austin Road towards East Tsim Sha Tsui. It's much easier if you ride the MTR and get off at the East Tsim Sha Tsui station and Exit in P2.

7. Clock Tower

The Clock Tower is located in the southern shore of Tsim Sha Tsui in Kowloon Peninsula near the Avenue of Stars. This landmark is historic because it is the only remaining original site of the Kowloon – Canton Railway. It was originally call the Kowloon – Canton Railway Clock

Chapter Six: Tourist Spots in Hong Kong

Tower and also referred as the Tsim Sha Tsui Clock Tower by the locals.

The Clock Tower reused the Pedder Street Clock Tower after it was demolished. In 1920, the 3 sides of the Clock Tower were installed and it began operating on March 22 1921, except during the Japanese occupation during World War II. The Clock Tower sustained damages from the war and up until now the marks of the combat is still visible.

The bell of the Clock Tower was moved inside it since 2010, but it was originally housed and displayed in Shatin Station from 1980's up to 1995.

The Clock Tower stand at about 44 meters and it is made out of red bricks and granite. There is a 7 meter long lightning rod on top of it. A wooden staircase is the only way tourists can reach the top of the tower. The interior is usually open for visitors especially tourists. In the year 2000, it is officially declared as a monument in Hong Kong.

If you want to go the historical Clock Tower, you can ride the MTR and get off in Tsim Sha Tsui Station and Exit in E. After which, take a 2 minute walk going to Salisbury Road, turn right, then take the subway near the Cultural Centre, then turn another right and walk on a straight path until you see the waterfront of the Clock Tower. Another option is riding the Star Ferry from Wan Chai or central, you can easily spot the Clock Tower because it is also near the Star Ferry Pier in Tsim Sha Tsui.

Chapter Six: Tourist Spots in Hong Kong

8. Ngong Ping 360

Ngong Ping 360 or sometimes called the aerial tramway is found in Lantau Island. It is created to improve tourism in Hong Kong which is why it is highly recommended that you try the going here for a ride and a tour around the area of Lantau. It was previously called the Tung Chung Cable Car Project before acquiring its recent name back in 2005. The Ngong Ping 360 experience is composed of the Ngong Ping Cable Car, Ngong Ping 360 Sky Rail and the Ngong Ping Village which is retail and entertainment area that is near the cable car's station.

Chapter Six: Tourist Spots in Hong Kong

The Ngong Ping 360 can bring you to the north coast of Lantau which is Tung Chung; Tung Chung is connected to Central Hong Kong. Before it was opened, the only access of to the mountain is through a bus.

The Ngong Ping cable car began construction in 2004 and was supposed to launch on January of 2006, however due to some technical and safety issues, the launching was moved at a later month. The Ngong Ping cable car was an alternative if you want to go to the Ngong Ping Plateau. Tourists and locals ride for about 25 minutes, while travelling a 5 kilometers distance from Tung Chung Bay to the Lantau Island.

The panoramic view of the South China Sea, North Lantau Park and even the Hong Kong International Airport going to the Po Lin Monastery above the terrains is truly breathtaking and a great visual experience for tourists and locals alike.

Part of the Ngong Ping 360 is the Ngong Ping Village, wherein traditional Chinese architectural designs are preserved. There are tons of shopping and dining places in this area as well as other attractions you can go to such as the Ngong Ping Tea House, Walking with Buddha and Monkeys Tale Theater.

The Ngong Ping 360 experience recently received an Enterprise Environmental Protection Achievement Award given by the Hong Kong Environmental Protection Association.

Chapter Six: Tourist Spots in Hong Kong

If you want to reach this cool place, just take the MTR and get off at Tung Chung Station and go to Exit B, then from there go to Ngong Ping bus terminal and board Bus 23. You can expect to arrive in about 1 hour. If you want a much quicker option while enjoying the view, from Tung Chung Station go to the Tung Chung Cable Car terminal, it will take about 30 minutes before you reach yet another cable car ride – the Ngong Ping Cable Car Terminal, from there it will take you to the Ngong Ping Island. I hope you are not afraid of heights!

Chapter Six: Tourist Spots in Hong Kong

9. Golden Bauhinia Square

The Golden Bauhinia Square, also known locally as the Golden Pak Choi, is another great way to interact with the city. It is located in Wan Chai, Hong Kong, just outside of the Hong Kong Convention and Exhibition Centre. The park was named after the golden statue of Bauhinia Blakeana, which is an important symbol for the people of Hong Kong after the handover.

If you are around the area especially during the Chinese New Year or the National Day of the People's Republic of China, there are spectacular firework shows as well as daily flag raising ceremonies followed by performances from the Police Pipe Band.

Chapter Six: Tourist Spots in Hong Kong

You can reach the Golden Bauhinia Square by taking the MTR (Wan Chai Station) and exit in Exit A5; you will reach the Central Plaza after walking in a footbridge for a few minutes. Once you reach the plaza, just continue walking until you reach the overhead walkway. Go down the ground level and you'll see the waterfront as well as the golden monument on the left side, the nearest landmark is the Hong Kong Convention and Exhibition Centre.

10. Victoria Harbour

Victoria Harbour is the lifeline of Hong Kong for centuries already. It is situated between the Central Hong Kong Island and the Kowloon Peninsula; it is the harbor that connects to main towns of Hong Kong. It has been crucial to

Chapter Six: Tourist Spots in Hong Kong

the British forces for a long time, and until today it still plays an important role in Hong Kong's economic development.

The Victoria Harbour has been constantly reclaimed for the past few years, although there were a lot of controversies about its reclamation, its functions remain the same – it is the major port for all international vessels, and the main domain in Hong Kong's busiest cities.

Back in 1850's, the harbor is famous for various water activities among the locals such as water polo, water races and variety of swimming competitions. The Victoria Recreation Club was also born because of this.

The Victoria Harbour started making its mark in history during the Taiping Rebellion that took place around 1854 – 1855. According to historians, the Chinese Imperial was attacked by large war boats of Taiping, and is engaging in a naval battle. However, the British forces ordered the Chinese Imperial to stop defending the harbor thus resulting in rising tension between the two nations; it resulted in a fight called the Arrow War. The Victoria Harbour was originally called the Hong Kong Harbour, but since the land at the time was under the Great Britain, it is renamed as Victoria Harbour in honor of Her Majesty Queen Victoria.

Today the Victoria Harbour is not just a port for various ships and ferries, it also serves as a great site and vantage point to view Hong Kong's amazing skyline, and breathtaking scenery where both tourists and locals can visually experience the famous symphony of lights at night,

Chapter Six: Tourist Spots in Hong Kong

and a space to share Hong Kong's culture and heritage during various festivals. The Victoria Harbour is perhaps the flagship symbol of Hong Kong. Its energy and invigorating atmosphere is what kept it vibrant throughout the years.

To get to the Victoria Harbour, just get off the MTR (East TST Station) in Exit L6. You won't miss it!

Chapter Seven: Temples in Hong Kong

When travelling in the different countries and cities of Asia, regardless of your religious background, it wouldn't be complete if you do not get to visit temples. You do not have to be a practicing and worshiping person in visiting temples. You can marvel at the beauty and the history that it has behind the architectural designs that can leave you speechless. Hong Kong has many beautiful temples that you can visit. This is a place where you can visit and marvel not only at the place of worship, but also appreciates the story behind why each temple was built. Not only those temples are a place of worship but it also houses a lot of extra

Chapter Seven: Temples in Hong Kong

services that can surely help you enjoy your visit. Here are 10 different temples you can visit when you are in Hong Kong.

1. Po Lin Monastery (Tian Tan Buddha)

Hidden away in lush mountains is the next famous destination in Hong Kong – the Po Lin Monastery which houses the biggest statue of Buddha in Hong Kong called Tian Tan Buddha (also known as Big Buddha or the Giant Buddha). Built in 1993, it stands at about 34 meters high and it is made out of majestic bronze. It is located in one of the most beautiful towns in Hong Kong – Ngong Ping, Lantau Island. The statue of the Big Buddha attracts over millions of tourists and pilgrims all over Asia. It is erected for the

Chapter Seven: Temples in Hong Kong

purpose of overlooking the Chinese people. The head including the eyes and lips as well as its right hand is raised to bless people and represents humility and dignity. The statue took about 12 years to complete.

Pilgrims should climb the grotto to reach the giant statue. The 268 steps are worth it once you get to the top, because of the breath taking view of the mountains and the South China Sea horizon.

The Po Lin Monastery is dubbed as the Buddhist World in the South; it is one of Hong Kong's renowned Buddhist sanctums because it is home to many devout monks, and it is a rich representation of Buddhism religion. Its garden is also filled with fresh flower scents and various birds surround the area.

There are also lots of vegetarian restaurants around the area that you can go to after trekking in one of the highest and largest statue in the world. You can also buy wooden bracelets that were made in the Po Lin Monastery and exclusively sold around the Tian Tan Buddha.

To get to Po Lin Monastery you can take the subway to Tung Chun Station. When you get there, take a bus called New Lantau Bus No.23 to Ngong Ping. Another way is that, at the Central Pier No. 6, you can take a ferry to Lantau Island. Then take the New Lantau Bus No.2 at the Mui Wi Bus station going to Ngong Ping.

Chapter Seven: Temples in Hong Kong

2. Ten Thousand Buddhas Temple

Another iconic and must go-to temple in Hong Kong is the Ten Thousand Buddhas Temple. This sacred monastery is found in Pai Tau Village, Sha Tin of the New Territories particularly in the Po Fook Hill. It is completed in 1957 and was founded in 1949 by Reverend Yuet Kai who is a devout Buddhist. The monastery however is not residential and it is only managed by lay people.

Chapter Seven: Temples in Hong Kong

You need to climb about 431 steps before you reached the pagoda (see photo) which is surrounded by gold Buddha statues. There are over 500 life-size gilded Arhan statues around the temple that is free for photo-ops. You can find the preserved corpse of Reverend Yuet Kai that is displayed in a monastery's main altar. Aside from the Pagoda, you can also check out the two pavilions, the four halls (higher level) and a tower (lower level). There are also various vegetarian restaurants around the area. The temple is free of charge for locals and tourists. Beware of fake monks who are begging for money, authentic monks are prohibited to beg for money.

To get to the Ten Thousand Buddha's temple take the MTR East Rail going to Sha Tin Station Exit B. Walk at the ramp alongside the bus terminal, down to street level. You will pass by Pai Tau Village on your left side. Continue walking until you reach Pai Tau Street (on your left). The landmark is the Grand Cental Plaza mall.

3. Man Mo Temple

Man Mo Temple is also known as the Wen Wu Temple. It is one of Hong Kong's famous temple and tourist spot that you should not miss especially if you are a devotee. It is located in Sheung Wan along the Hollywood Road.

The Man Mo Temple is a tribute to the God of Literature (Man) and the God of War (Mo). It is believed that these two "gods" were worshipped and patronize by students who wanted to succeed in civil examinations of Imperial China. The civil examination is aimed at finding the best officials for the state. Students also go here to pray and ask guidance for their studies.

The temple is built around 1847, and it is the largest Man Mo temple in Hong Kong. Locals and even tourists,

Chapter Seven: Temples in Hong Kong

pause for a moment to contemplate under the several giant hanging incense coils. Around Man Mo temple, tourists can also check out Lit Shing Kung (worship for all the heavenly gods) and Kung Sor (assembly hall) where community affairs or disputes are debated and discussed.

The Man Mo temple is under the management of Tung Wah Group of Hospitals since 1908, and in 2009 it is officially listed as a Grade I historic building and a declared monument.

If you want to go to this place, you can ride the MTR (Sheung Wan Station) until you get to the Hollywood Road via the Ladder Street.

To get to Ma Mon temple, you'd have to walk towards The Center along Queen's Road Central. Go to the Central Mid-Levels Escalator which will take you to Hollywood road. At MTR Sheung Wan Station Exit A2. Walk along the Hilliet Street which will lead to Queen's Road Central. Go to the Ladder Street (which is next to Lok Ku Road) to Hollywood Road and then to the Man Mo Temple.

4. Che Kung Temple

Situated in Tai Wai area of Sha Tin is Che Kung Temple. It was made in honor of Che Kung, a military commander of the Southern Song dynasty in the year 1127 to 1279. He was known of having a great power in restraining rebellion at their time. According to some folklore, he was the one who helped Prince Ping and his brother to the South, in Sai Kung, in order to keep the Song State alive. He was not just looked up to as a great military commander, but eventually was revered to as a god because of the achievements that he has brought.

In 1338 – 1644, the end of the Ming dynasty is when the original temple was built. It was renovated in the year

Chapter Seven: Temples in Hong Kong

1890, 1993 and 2004. The renovation that happened in 1993 was made to make sure that the temple accommodates the increasing number of worshippers in the second day of Chinese New Year which the Che Kung Festival is celebrated which is also his birthday.

    The giant statue of Che Kung can be found at the altar of the main worship hall. That main hall is edged by a huge drum and bell. A wheel of fortune is also situated there which is believed to bring in good luck when you walk around it for 3 times. To get to the Che Kung temple, you need to ride the MTR Che Kung Temple Station Exit B.

Chapter Seven: Temples in Hong Kong

5. Chi Lin Nunnery and Nan Lian Garden

Located in Diamond Hill, Kowloon is the Chin Lin Nunnery. It is a beautiful temple with an elegant wooden design. It was instituted in the year 1934 and was renovated in AD 618-907 in the Tang dynasty manner. It is a Buddhist temple which has statues of the goddess of mercy Guanyin, bodhisttvas and Sakyamuni Buddha. The statues are made from various materials like gold, clay, wood and stone.

As it was said, the nunnery was renovated in the Tang Dynasty which explains why the design of temple is based on Sukhavati drawing in Magao Caves. What is amazing about this architecture is that no nails were used though it is constructed with cypress wood which uses the traditional Chinese architectural techniques to make it happen. It is the largest hand-made wooden building all over the world.

Opposite to the Chin Lin Nunnery is the Nan Lian Garden which is a Chinese Classical garden. It was built in accordance to the style of the Tang dynasty. Every detail in this 3.5 hectares lot was designed according to specific rules and methods. You can also check out the teahouse and vegetarian restaurant in this place.

To get to this place, take the MTR Diamond Hill Station Exit 2. From there you can follow the signs and just stroll around 5 minutes until you reach your destination.

Chapter Seven: Temples in Hong Kong

6. *Fung Ying Seen Koon*

Fung Ying Seen Koon is located in Fanling, New Territories which is a Taoist temple founded in 1929. This temple is named after Fung Lau and Ying Chau which are two fairy islands. They believe that these fairy isalands are inhabited by immortals.

This place is eye catching because of its structure which has a hillside location. The temple has a traditional Chinese design which has an orange-tiled roof and red pillars of stone. It is said that in terms of Daoist craftsmanship and design, this temple is a great example. Theses beautifully crafted architectures makes visitors and tourist want to examine every detail of it.

Chapter Seven: Temples in Hong Kong

Situated there are different temples. The Grand temple is dedicated for the worship of Taishang Laojun, Lu Dongbin, Qui Chuji. Laojun is known to be one of the highest deities of Daoism. Another temple is the Guanyin Temple that was made to worship Guanyin in respect with his compassion and deity of mercy. On the other hand, Yuen San Temple is established for the sixty Great Generals of the Chinese sexagesimal cycle and Doumu, the deity of medicine, healing, fertility and nurture. You can also find The Colorful Sculpture of "Yellow Emperor Inquiries after the Tai" which displays the trip of Guangchenzi to Mt. Kongdong. Lastly, you can also find the craving of the "Scroll of Eighty-Seven Immortals" which represents China's pride on classical portraits and drawing techniques. Just like other temples, a vegetarian canteen serves food for the public.

To get to Fung Yin Seen Kong, you can take the MTR to Fanling Station Exit B. Look for the orange double roofs of the temple; the walk will take about 5 minutes to reach the destination.

Chapter Seven: Temples in Hong Kong

7. *Kwan Kung Pavilion*

The Kwan Kung Pavilion is located at Cheung Chau Island at Hong Kong. The temple was built in the year 1973. The temple was dedicated for Kwan Kung, the god of war and wealth. This temple houses the eight feet statue of Kwan Kung of the Hand Dynasty in 206 BC to 220 AD). His sword called the Kwan Dou is also found in the temple.

The statue of Kwan Kung is made entirely of camphor tree which makes it special. When you enter the temple, you can find a pavilion and in front of it is an incense burner with two dragons. The cherry blossoms bloom in the month of March that wonderfully covers the temples with color and a sweet aroma.

Chapter Seven: Temples in Hong Kong

To get to the Kwan Kung Temple, walk from the Cheung Chau Ferry Piet to Cheung Chau Beach Road headed for Warwick Hotel. When you reach that, turn to the Cheung Chau Sports Road then walk to Kwun Yam Wan Road.

8. Seven Sisters Temple

The Seven Sisters Temple is located at Pak Wan, Peng Chau, and Outlaying Islands. It is constructed in the year 1954. The name "seven sisters" came from a fabled weaving maid who is the daughter of the queen mother. She envied the world outside her so-called-world. In secret, she permits a pigeon to fly down to the earth but eventually the pigeon

Chapter Seven: Temples in Hong Kong

was chased by an eagle, but there came a cow-herder to rescue it. To thank him, she agreed to marry him. The couple was very happy but there weren't thriving because the maid stopped weaving. As a punishment, the grandmother she separated the cow-herder and their children from the maid. But, eventually the grandmother was moved by the weeping of the children and so she made the magpies fly to create a bridge in the riverbank to reunite the family.

This day is the seventh day of the seventh month of the lunar calendar that is why the Seven Sister Festival is celebrated that day. The temple was not only made to honor the sisters, but it was also made to help women in enhancing their needlecraft. They also help out couples who desire to have a family of their own.

To get to the Seven Sisters Temple, in the Peng Chau Ferry, turn left and walk for about 5 minutes to reach Peng Chau Waterfront Playground. When you get there, turn right to Peng Lei Road and walk for about 5 minutes to reach your destination.

Chapter Seven: Temples in Hong Kong

9. Golden Flower Shrine

Within the lane neighboring to Peng Chau Wing on Street is the Golden Flower Shrine. This temple is known to bestow honor to the Goddess Golden Flower. They believe that the goddess Golden Flower can grant numerous generations of descendants. The popular Bodhisatta Festival is celebrated all together with the festival of the goddess of the Golden Flower.

Chapter Seven: Temples in Hong Kong

It is in the 17th day of the fourth month of the lunar calendar that her festival is celebrated. Stories from long ago say that a famous Cantonese opera performer named Tak-hing and the head priest of the temple met the goddess in their dreams. They believe that on her festival day, dragons of different colors and lions dances as the temple comes to life.

In the year 1762 during the Qing Dynasty, a herbalist, Lai Guo Wen, needed medicine so that his wife can be treated with the sickness that she has. To thank Madame Jinhua of the wish granted to him, he built a temple which is still up until this time of the day.

To get to the Golden Flower Shrine, you need to go to the Peng Chau Ferry Pier to the Peng Chau Wing Street. From there, turn left at the Tin Hau Temple. Right in to the adjacent lane; turn right in Peng Chau Wing on Street.

10. Hau Wong Temple

Most of the temples are named after whom it is dedicated to. Hau Wong temple however is not a name of a person, but it is term that can be translated to Prince Marquis. Hau Wong is often referred to a courageous and loyal general named Yeung Leung-jit. He was an army man who protected the last emperor of the Southern Song Dynasty though his health was deteriorating.

People believed that there were conflicting theories of the temple's origin. Another theory of explaining the legend of this temple is that, the temple was made for a resident that cured the emperor of Song from a certain illness.

Chapter Seven: Temples in Hong Kong

Of the two theories of origin, it seems that Hau Wong won because facing the temple's entrance hall is an image of him. The temple is not only a place of worship, but it also houses different cultural artifacts, reliefs on the wall, Chinese calligraphy and numerous plaques. There is also a iron incense in the temple which is burned and dedicated to Hau Wong. You can also find Shek Wan pottery, and walls ornamented with colorful figurines.

To get to the Hau Wong Temple, take the MTR to Lok Fu Station Exit B. When you reach the station, you can start following the signs on the way to Hau Wong temple. This walk to the temple from the station will take about 10 minutes.

Chapter Eight: Interacting with Hong Kong

If the different tourist attractions are not enough for you, then maybe you need a little more adventure and immersion to truly appreciate what Hong Kong has to offer. One way of doing that is by interacting not only with its places but also the people and culture embedded within.

In this chapter, we have put together 10 of the best things you need to try and do while you are in Hong Kong. Some of these places are also great tourist destinations wherein you can enjoy and get to know the people, the culture and Hong Kong's way of life through the eyes of a local.

Chapter Eight: Interacting with Hong Kong

1. *Star Ferry Ride*

The Star Ferry is a passenger double-decker ferry that carries tourists and locals who wanted to sail across the Victoria Harbour from the Hong Kong Island to the Kowloon Peninsula. It was founded in 1888, and has since then carried about 70,000 passengers a day; riding the popular ferry is one of the ways for you to enjoy Hong Kong's most iconic Victoria Harbour!

The Star Ferry is consists of 12 ferries that are operating daily in two routes - Central and Tsim Sha Tsui. Even if you can cross to the other side through buses or trains, tourists still preferred to ride the Star Ferry because

Chapter Eight: Interacting with Hong Kong

aside from the sightseeing experience, it is one of the cheapest ways to get to the other side of the city.

Let me give you a quick background on how Star Ferry became one of the iconic rides you shouldn't dare miss while you are in Hong Kong. It all started in 1870, when a British man by the name of Grant Smith brought a wooden boat that would ran back and forth at different intervals across the Victoria Harbour.

Few years before the steam ferry was created people use the sampans to cross the harbor. About three years after Grant Smith attempted to run steam ferries from Hong Kong Island to the Kowloon Peninsula, the British consul in Canton briefly stopped the operation because it might cause people to reach the gambling houses in Kowloon. So in 1888, a man named Dorabjee Naorojee Mithaiwala founded a ferry company known as the "Kowloon Ferry Company." He bought the boat by Grant Smith and further developed it, and because of the ferries popularity, he was able to acquire four more new vessels; the Morning Star, Rising Star, Guiding Star and the Evening Star. These vessels had a 100 seating capacity and were making about 147 trips a day. By 1898, he incorporated the company changing its name to Star Ferry Co Ltd.

Fast forward in 1933, the Star Ferry company created the first ever diesel operated electric passenger ferry called the Electric Star.

Chapter Eight: Interacting with Hong Kong

During the Japanese Occupation, the Star Ferry particularly the Golden and Meridian Star was used to transport prisoners of war, the Electric Star was later bombed by the Americans and sunk in the harbor, but after the war, the vessels were recovered and were operational until today.

The Star Ferry is celebrating its 119th year as one of the main means of public transportation in Hong Kong. It was officially declared by the Society of American Travel Writers as one of the Top 10 Most Exciting Ferry Rides back in 2009.

Here's how you can get to the Star Ferry piers or stations; to get to the TST Star Ferry pier, take an MTR to Tsim Sha Tsui Station Exit L6. Just walk along Salisbury Road to the Clock Tower.

If you wanted to start the ride in the Central Star Ferry, take the MTR to Hong Kong Station A2 Exit A. You can walk to the pier along Man Yiu Street.

Lastly, to get to Wan Chai Ferry Station, take the MTR to Wan Chai Station Exit A1. From there, you can ride the sky bridge to the Hong Kong Convention and Exhibition Center then go down to the Convention Avenue at the Harbour Road.

Chapter Eight: Interacting with Hong Kong

2. *Duk Ling Ride*

Do you want to have a different kind of ride across the harbor – Chinese style? Then Duk Ling ride is for you! Duk Ling is an authentic Chinese junk that is mainly used to travel along the Hong Kong waterways, which were owned by Chinese fishermen for a very long time. In the year 2015, after about 60 years, the Duk Ling boats were restored to its original design.

The sailing of the Duk Ling ride were at first offered two times a week in the Victoria Harbour for tours. This was manned by the Hong Kong Tourism board. At first, the sailings were free of charge, but eventually they charged $50

Chapter Eight: Interacting with Hong Kong

HK and were later increased to $100 HK. But in the year 2014, the Hong Kong Tourist board trips were ceased.

A year later, the sailing tours resumed following the Set Sail Ceremony. Now, for HK$230 (per person) you can enjoy a 45 minute ride cruising across the Victoria Harbour. If you are with your kids or you are a Senior Citizen, it will only cost you HK $160. That's a huge discount!

The Duk Ling is not limited to sailing the Victoria Harbour for tours, it was also used to cruise the Lamma Island, Po Toi and Lei Yue Mun. It can also be used for a romantic place to celebrate weddings and anniversary receptions.

Duk Ling has a daily ride offering that has different times of pick up points; its terminal is in mainly two locations – the Kowloon Public Pier 3 at Tsim Sha Tsui and in Central Pier 9.

You can catch a ride at the Kowloon Public Pier 3, Tsim Sha Tsui with one hour intervals starting from 2:30 PM until 8:30 PM. You can also try in the Central Pier 9, the pickup starts at 2:45 PM with one hour intervals until 8:45 PM.

3. Hong Kong Space Museum

Nerds out there listen up! If you love space and you are into astronomy, then the Hong Kong Space Museum is a must-see for you! It is located in Tsam Sha Tsui and was opened to the public since 1980. The planetarium has two wings – the east and west. The east wing is a dome structure that is shaped like an egg. You can find the Stanley Ho Space Theatre as well as the Hall of Space Science in the east wing. The west wing, on the other hand, houses the Lecture Hall, the Hall of Astronomy, as well as some offices and a gift shop of souvenirs.

Chapter Eight: Interacting with Hong Kong

The Hong Kong Space museum is a famous landmark and the first local planetarium of space and astronomy in the city; it also covers more than 8,000 square meters. You can also find a mock up cockpit section of the Space Shuttle orbiter used in NASA. The two major exhibits that you can go to if you want to learn and be entertained are the Hall of Space Science and the Hall of Astronomy.

Here's how you can get there - just take the MTR to the East Tsim Sha Tsui Station Exit J. From there, there is approximately a 10 minute walk to the museum.

4. Hong Kong Cultural Centre

Chapter Eight: Interacting with Hong Kong

The Hong Kong Cultural Centre is a multipurpose performance facility that was founded by the Urban Council but was later on transferred to the Hong Kong Government and administered by the Leisure and Cultural Services Department. It is located in Tsim Sha Tsui particularly in Salisbury Road.

The Cultural Center has 3 different theaters; first is the Concert hall, it has a 2,000 seating capacity. The auditorium in Concert hall is oval shaped and two tiered. The Hong Kong Cultural Center houses the largest pipe-organ in Asia (8,000 pipes), that's why the Hong Kong Philharmonic orchestra always performs there.

The second theatre you can find is the Grand Theater. It has a seating capacity of about 1,730. It is mostly used for ballets, musicals, and large scale operas, that is why it is designed as a three-tiered auditorium. The third theatre is called the Studio Theatre which has a 300 to 490 seating capacity. The Hong Kong Cultural Center is located at Tsim Sha Tsui which is adjacent to Star Ferry on the west. Adjacent to the east is the Hong Kong Space Museum and the Hong Kong Museum of Art. You can easily find it once you get to TST.

5. Lin Heung Tea House

Food savvy people out there can never say no to Chinese food or in this case, a beverage, because of one reason: its authenticity. Located at Wellington Street corner Aberdeen Street is a Chinese Restaurant founded in Guangzhou, China called Lin Heung Tea House.

In the first years of the 20th century, tea houses began to flourish in China. One of them is the Lin Heung Tea House, which later on opened two more branches in Mong Kok and Central Hong Kong Island around 1926. In 1980, the tea house made its transition in its current location.

Chapter Eight: Interacting with Hong Kong

After years of thriving in the business, it has gained the attention of CNN and Times Magazine and was also featured in several movies mainly because of their famous traditional dumplings that are always sought after by locals and tourists. When you dine in at the Lin Heung Tea House, the visual aspects of the place will take you to a trip down memory lane because Dim Sum is served on traditional trolleys. Authenticity at its best indeed!

The tea house also offers variety of food in their menu like Pa Wong Duck, Stuff Mud Carp, Whole Winter Melon Soup, Steamed Chicken Bun and Shumai made with Liver, which you can never find that in any other Chinese restaurant.

If you want to check out the Lin Heung Tea House, just take the MTR to Sheung Wan Station Exit 2. It is located exactly in 102 Wellington Street Central, Hong Kong.

Chapter Eight: Interacting with Hong Kong

6. Madame Tussauds Hong Kong

The west, without a doubt also has influenced the east especially when it comes to all things Hollywood! In the Peak Tower of Hong Kong Island is a wax museum called Madame Tussauds Hong Kong, which was founded by Marie Tussaud, hence its name. The wax museum in Hong Kong is the first in Asia. Of course, there is only one big difference, instead of seeing the life-size wax figure of Brad Pitt, you'll see Jackie Chan! Well let's just say he is the 'Brad Pitt of China'

The wax figures of nearly 100 different personalities and popular Chinese stars are housed in this museum, and since it is located in Asia, one third of the total number of

Chapter Eight: Interacting with Hong Kong

wax figures are Asian artists. The wax figures in Madame Tussauds' Hong Kong features different themes like the World Premier, Music Icons, Historical and National Heroes, The Champions and the Hong Kong Glamour.

Madam Tussauds Hong Kong opened in the year 2000. They decided to open a branch in Hong Kong because the city caters to different Asian Markets which makes it accessible for people and Asian tourists. Madam Tussauds' can also be found in prestigious cities like London, Las Vegas, Amsterdam, New York, Los Angeles and other major cities in the world.

You can take the mini bus, taxi or the Peak Tram to get to Madam Tussauds' Hong Kong. Entrance fee costs only HK $140 for adults and HK $70 for children (3-11 years old) and it is opened all year round.

Chapter Eight: Interacting with Hong Kong

7. *Hong Kong Wet Land Park*

Nature lovers out there, prepare to experience paradise! "Unroll the Hong Kong Diverse Green Temptations" is the slogan of the Hong Kong Wetland Park. It is a tourism, conservation and educational facility located in the northern part of Tin Shui Wai, Yuen Long. The place is a 10,000 square meter visitor center with a 60-hectre Wetland reserve.

In the year 1998, a research was made by the Agriculture, Fisheries and Conversation Department as well as the Hong Kong Tourism Board. They were conducting a feasibility

Chapter Eight: Interacting with Hong Kong

study for a wetland park to be made without compromising the land to build a wetland ecotourism attraction. To be able to preserve and conserve the land, they re-created habitats for the wildlife. Other facilities such as Mangrove Boardwalk, Stream Walk, Succession Walk and many more can be found here. In 2007, they won an excellence award at the Asia Pacific Competition.

For you to get to the Hong Kong Wet Land Park, you can take the MTR Light Rail in the Zone 5A stop for a single ride ticket. Routes are listed below:

- 705 – Tin Wai Circular (Counter-Clockwise)
- 706 – Tin Shui Wai Ciruclar (Clockwise)
- 761P: Yuen Long to Tin Wing (departing every 13 minutes starting from 10:00 to 15:00 every day)

Chapter Eight: Interacting with Hong Kong

8. Hong Kong Museum of Art

The Hong Kong Museum of Art is unlike any other art museums in Hong Kong. This museum regularly changes its displays. The museum is composed of different paintings, sculptures, and calligraphy from China, Hong Kong and different parts of the world.

The museum is currently located in Salisbury Road; however the art museum has transferred from one location to another. Around 1975, the Hong Kong Museum of History and the Hong Kong Museum of art was split into two. The premise of the museum at the present time has

Chapter Eight: Interacting with Hong Kong

been its home since 1991. It is undergoing renovation every now and then so that tourists can have a better experience of Asian arts.

If you are an artsy type of person then the Hong Kong Art Museum is definitely for you. To get there just take the MTR to the East Tsim Sha Station and Tsim Sha Tsui Station. From there, you can walk towards the museum; it will probably be a 10 minute walk from the train station.

9. *Yau Ma Tei Theatre*

For those who loves theatre and arts particularly Chinese films, you should check out the Yau Ma Tei Theatre.

Chapter Eight: Interacting with Hong Kong

It is located in the Yau Tsim Mong District, south of Kowloon Peninsula. It is also known as 'Waterloo' which was named after the Waterloo Road. It is the only cinema and theatre facility that survived after the World War II.

Yau Ma Tei Theatre was listed as a historic building in the year 1998, and was closed down that same year but was again reprised in 2012 for what it was made for. The theatre was enthusiastic about showing Cantonese opera which also comes with English subtitles.

For movie lovers out there, just take the MTR to Yau Ma Tei Station, Exit B2. From there, you can walk along the Waterloo Road. It will take you about 5 minutes to reach the Reclamation Road. Enjoy!

Chapter Eight: Interacting with Hong Kong

10. Arts in the Park Mardi Gras

In 2001, Hong Kong adopted yet another western tradition called the Arts in the Park Mardi Gras. It is inspired by the international art festivals in United States as well as Rio de Janeiro Carnival in Brazil, and the Nothing Hill Carnival in London. It is an annual event in which there is a showcase of beautiful masterpieces where people can come and just experience this great display of visual arts. Students and locals are the art contributors for this event.

This outdoor gallery does not only show visual arts but there are also live performances when you come and visit. Stalls of beautiful crafted art are displayed which includes giant puppets and display floats. Not only can you see these great exhibits, but you can also be a part of it. Head dresses, masks, rod puppet and face painting can be made and tried for free! It's a fun artsy party for the family.

Chapter Eight: Interacting with Hong Kong

The annual event happens in the month of November. The arts event lasts for 2 days from 10 AM in the morning until 5 PM. It is held at the Central Law, Victoria Park. Schedules may vary each year so be sure to check out their website and stay tune for event updates at: <www.hkyaf.com>

Chapter Nine: Nightlife in Hong Kong

Another best way to experience Hong Kong is during night time. Hong Kong offers a variety of choices on how to enjoy the night life that aren't just limited in going to clubs or bars. You can have lots of options where you can relax, enjoy and have the best time with your family and loved ones.

Night life in Hong Kong is all about shopping, clubbing (Chinese style), relaxing, touring, watching race courses, flying in heli-tours and more! Here are 10 different ways on how you can spend the night in your stay at Hong Kong.

Chapter Nine: Nightlife in Hong Kong

1. *Symphony of Lights*

First stop is a pyrotechnical show called - Symphony of Lights. It is the world's largest permanent light and sound show according to Guinness World Records. If you truly want to see the city's amazing skyline overlooking the Victoria Harbour then stay tune every night for this! Best part is that it is a daily light and sound show in Hong Kong that happens at 8 PM, so you'll never worry about missing it!

The Hong Kong Tourism Board organized the show which lasts for about 14 minutes, different companies

Chapter Nine: Nightlife in Hong Kong

participates every night to showcase their own skyscrapers. The symphony of lights is conceptualized, created, and installed by Laservision. The orchestration of music, decoration lights, laser light displays, and pyrotechnic fireworks are featured in this multimedia light and sound show.

The Avenue of Stars on the Tsim Sha Tsui waterfront or the waterfront promenade outside the Golden Bauhinia Square in Wan Chai and on sightseeing ferries such as the Star Ferry running across the Victoria Harbour are best vantage points that you could utilize in seeing the show. The promenade outside the Golden Bauhinia Square in Wan Chai is held every night and the show's music and narration is also live at the Avenue of Stars.

The narration is in Cantonese on Sundays, Mondays, and Wednesdays. English narrations is scheduled on Fridays, while it is in Mandarin on Tuesdays, Thursdays.

Special pyrotechnic fireworks are also added to the show on the rooftop of participating buildings on both sides of the harbor or at the Tsim Sha Tsui waterfront. It is used on special events or holidays, like Chinese New Year and Christmas.

The show is automatically suspended, if there is a Tropical Cyclone Warning Signal No.3 or above a Red or Black Rainstorm Warning Signal as issued by the Hong Kong Observatory at or after 3 pm on any given day.

Chapter Nine: Nightlife in Hong Kong

It will also be suspended in emergencies without prior notice. So if you think that a storm is coming, don't expect to see the buildings light up.

To get a great spot in watching the showcase of these lights, you can take the MTR to East Tsim Sha Tsui Station, Exit L6. From there you can walk for about 5 minutes to reach the Hong Kong Cultural Centre.

2. Victoria Harbour Square Cruise

Hong Kong's magnificent skyline at dusk is so beautiful that even locals can't get enough of it! When it casts in hues of orange and pink, the sky line looks incredibly serene, and it continues to bubble with action like recently popped

Chapter Nine: Nightlife in Hong Kong

champagne. From the water on board a Hong Kong evening harbor cruise to the wonderful panorama of the view, you will surely enjoy the ride!

The 'Shining Star' ferry, a recreation of the ferries that graced Victoria Harbour since the twenties sailed back in time to Hong Kong today as a beautiful double-decker ferry. You can't help but soak yourself in the magnificent views of the evening sea breeze which would whisk your mind away!

The tour of Star Ferry is a single ride night round trip which would pass the following destinations: Sheung Wan, Central, Wan Chai, Causeway Bay and Tsim Sha Tsui. You do not have to worry about the commentary because some of the commentary you would encounter would include English and Mandarin.

Take note that the departure time of the ferry varies for a particular period; from February 1 to September 30, departure time is around 7 PM. From January 31 to October 1, departure time is usually 6 PM.

The pick-up points of the Star Ferry are in Star Ferry Pier in Tsim Sha Tsui, Central Pier 7, and Wan Chai Ferry Pier. The duration of the whole trip would approximately last an hour which would cost about HK$180 for adults, HK$162 for children that are 3 to 12 years old or seniors that are aged 65 and above as well as disabled persons.

You should buy tickets 10 minutes prior to boarding the cruise.

Chapter Nine: Nightlife in Hong Kong

3. *Aberdeen Harbour Night*

If for some reason, you are already sick of all things Victoria Harbour (I mean, why would you?) Then I guess, it's time for a new sight that will still dazzle your senses at night! I'm talking about Hong Kong's Aberdeen Harbour.

This is where you can find the Jumbo Floating Restaurant particularly in the shores of Aberdeen fishing village, it is one of Hong Kong's most renowned eateries. You could indulge yourself to a delicious feast, or take a stroll along the harbor where you can work up your appetite.

There are night cruises that Water Tours provide with an itinerary of pre-dinner cocktail cruise around Aberdeen

Chapter Nine: Nightlife in Hong Kong

Harbour, dinner at Jumbo Floating Restaurant and Stubb's Road Lookout. The departure time would be more specific when you have made your booking though you would be fetched at around 5:15 PM. The duration of the cruise would last approximately 4 hours which would cost you HK$900 for adults and HK$770 for children ages 12 and below. The pickup points for the Water Tour at Aberdeen Harbour are at Pier 9 and the Kowloon Public Pier, Tsim Sha Tsui.

4. Temple Street Night Market

I've mentioned lots of shopping districts in previous chapters, but I purposely saved the Temple Night Market for

Chapter Nine: Nightlife in Hong Kong

this list, simply because locals and tourists really loved shopping here at night for aesthetical reasons. The Temple Street Night Market is located in Yau Ma Tei in Kowloon. It is the busiest flea markets at night in the territory; it is also common to see the place crowded at dusk.

The place is also known as "Men's street" as it is popular for men's fashion though you could also buy clothes for women and children as well as cheap merchandise and food items. The place was built during the Qing Dynasty, and it was named after Tin Hau temple which is also built on the street.

The market is lively at dusk daily and usually starts at 2 PM. There are more than a hundred stalls—that sell items mainly for men, jeans, t-shirts, pants, lighters, shoes, condoms and men's accessories—with colorful lights in the market. There are also carts bulging with goods from clothing to mobile phones and watches. Prices can always be negotiated for items that are cheap second hand goods like cassettes, video tapes, old newspapers, antiques, etc.

This is for the "Indian Jones" of fashion because it is advised that one should hunt for shops hidden in the streets behind the stalls when buying merchandise in Temple Street. It's like you are searching for gold! You could also shop and enjoy a Cantonese opera show.

The Temple Street Night market is located at Jordan Road and Kansu Street.

Chapter Nine: Nightlife in Hong Kong

For all you shopaholics, you can take the MTR to Yau Ma Tei Station, Exit C. Then turn to Temple Street located at Man Ming lane. Another alternative route is you can take the MTR to Jordan Statio, Exit A. Then you can turn right to Jordan road and turn right again on Temple Street.

5. *Heli-Tour in Hong Kong*

This next night activity is not for everyone, exclusive for rich people only! Unless you happen to win a jackpot price in the lottery – welcome aboard!

Chapter Nine: Nightlife in Hong Kong

If you like to experience Hong Kong from a bird's eye view perspective especially at night time, then why not try to fly and dine or just relax as you travel the beautiful sky aboard a helicopter!

Enjoy the stunning Hong Kong landscape with "flight-seeing tour." The journey begins at the China Clipper, an exclusive lounge located on the 30th floor of The Peninsula Hong Kong, offering spectacular harbor views. The tour offers pilot commentaries of the areas being viewed, allowing you to enjoy a completely different perspective of the city.

No children under the age of two shall be carried unless they are secured in an approved child seatbelt. Please note that a helicopter service has no child seatbelt available at this time.

The Peninsula Hong Kong can be found at Salisbury Road. To get there, you can take the MTR to East Tsim Sha Tsui, Exit J and walk to the hotel.

Chapter Nine: Nightlife in Hong Kong

6. *Lan Kwai Fong Bars and Pubs*

Night life will never be memorable without some drinks and good stories in between! Of course, bars and clubs will never be out of the picture (unless your kids are with you – drink responsibly!)

Lan Kwai Fong in Central Hong Kong houses lots of different bars and clubs that keep the dance floor moving all night long. This part of the city makes you feel the youthful vibe with exhilarating sounds and lights.

Here are some of the best nightclubs at Lan Kwai Fong that will surely give you a memorable nightlife with dear friends or even local strangers:

Chapter Nine: Nightlife in Hong Kong

- Volar
- Dragon
- Magnum
- Tasmania Ballroom

All these night clubs are found along the streets of Lan Kwai Fong. So for all the party goers out there, just take the MTR Central Station, Exit D2. Then you can walk along the Theatre Lane up to D'Aguilar Street. Bottom's up!

7. Western and Chinese Night Clubs

If bars and pubs are not enough, why don't you try partying like a Chinese? The best part is it is for the whole family! (Unlike bars and pubs – only for "matured people")

Chapter Nine: Nightlife in Hong Kong

Western or Chinese are the two flavors of nightclubs in Hong Kong. This is suited for both business purposes and family entertainment. You can add dining packages and drinks as well.

Singing, acrobatic exhibitions, folk dances, and Cantonese operas are one of the performances that you will encounter in the nightclubs. All other events have merged into the sumptuous banquet of Hong Kong's nightlife like Hong Kong's film, nightclub, bars and pubs, music and drama. Experience the dynamic charm of this Oriental Pearl by jumping into the rush! You and your family will surely have a good time.

Tsim Sha Tsui is the place where you can find Western and Chinese night clubs. Just take the MTR to East Tsim Sha Tsui, Exit J and walk to find the night clubs. You will not miss it (judging by the amount of light in its establishments).

Chapter Nine: Nightlife in Hong Kong

8. *Happy Valley Race Course*

The Happy Valley Racecourse is one of the two racecourses for horse racing and is a tourist attraction in Hong Kong. The race course has a 55,000 seating capacity. It is located in Happy Valley on Hong Kong Island and near the Wong Nai Chung Road and Morrison Hill Road,

The Happy Valley, built in 1845, was made to provide horse racing for the British residing in Hong Kong. The first race happened in1846. It is the only flat ground suitable for horse racing on Hong Kong Island, it is a reclaimed area.

The Hong Kong Government prohibited rice growing by villages in the surrounding area to make way for the

Chapter Nine: Nightlife in Hong Kong

racecourse. As time went on horse racing became more and more popular among the Chinese residents and tourists alike.

The race track was rebuilt in 1995 and it is now considered a world-class horse racing facility.

The Happy Valley Racecourse is used by the Hong Kong Jockey Club for horse racing competitions and events. It is open to the public as well as members of the Club; the Happy Valley race takes place every Wednesday nights.

A seven-story facility, capable of accommodating approximately 55,000 spectators is also home for other sporting events such as football, hockey and rugby. It also has various leisure facilities managed by the Leisure and Cultural Services Department.

Races are usually held at the month of September to July, every Wednesday evenings at 7:30 PM. Admission fee is HK $10 and people below 18 years old are not allowed to enter.

For horse lovers and sports enthusiasts out there, just take the MTR to Causeway Bay and follow the signs to get to the racecourse. You can also take the Happy Valley Tram through the Wong Nai Chung Road.

Chapter Nine: Nightlife in Hong Kong

9. Opera House Hong Kong

Musical fans unite! If you are looking for something classy and educational, then buy ticket and watch classic Chinese and Asian opera shows at the Opera Hong Kong. The institution was established in 2003 by Warren Mok, a famous opera singer in Hong Kong, it is co-founded with other opera lovers. The Opera Hong Kong aims to develop and increase the people's appreciation of the opera. They are committed to promoting the talent of the locals themselves. The Opera Hong Kong was recognized by the public in 2008.

Chapter Nine: Nightlife in Hong Kong

Not only did Opera Hong Kong produce good and quality operas and concerts, but they also offer educational programs. These educational programs aim to reach young people by teaching them an art that can be very encouraging and inspiring to watch.

To find more information about the Opera Hong Kong, you can visit their website at <www.operahongkong.com> for their upcoming shows and concerts.

10. Intercontinental Infinity Pools

If going out at night is not your cup of tea. Don't worry! you can still enjoy a lovely evening while relaxing by the

Chapter Nine: Nightlife in Hong Kong

infinity pools of the Intercontinental Hotel. You can rest your eyes in an awe-inspiring view of the Victoria Harbour.

The hotel has a large outdoor swimming pool which is very much unique with its infinity design. A breathtaking view and spa pools are the perfect combination of a relaxing way to spend your night without going through the hassles of Hong Kong.

The infinity pool of the Intercontinental Hotel is located at the 3rd floor which is open from 8 AM to 10 PM. They also serve food and they also have a full beverage service. The access of the infinity pool is limited only to the guest in-residence and the members of Club I-SPA.

The hotel is situated in Mody Road, Tsim Sha Tsui East Kowloon. To get there, you can take the MTR to East Tsim Sha Tsui, Exit J and you can follow the signs leading to the hotel. But keep in mind; you have to stay here for a night or two to access the infinity pool, nevertheless, it will be a great way to spend your nigh away.

Chapter Ten: Off Hong Kong's Beaten Path

Sometimes the best things are not easily seen by many. When it comes to travelling, not all the popular places are the only ones that are worth the visit. Beaten paths are to be discovered because you'll never know what you'll find and experience in those places.

Hong Kong is a place where you can find not just the city's popular tourist attractions, but also the beautiful places that are mostly not at the top of the list or not on the list at all when you are planning to travel a city or a country. Here are 10 places you should dare discover yourself, this off beaten path that will surely make you appreciate Hong Kong and look at it from a different perspective.

Chapter Ten: Off Hong Kong's Beaten Path

1. Tai O Fishing Village

First stop is what the locals called the "Venice of Hong Kong." As you can see on the photo above, the boats and the river setting of this village really reminds you of Venice in Italy. The Tai O fishing village is located in the western side of Lantau Island, and its name means large inlet which refers to the Tai O Creek and the Tai O River outlet.

When the British forces were in Hong Kong, the village was known as Tanka Village, and it became an entry point for illegal immigrants escaping from mainland China. Tai O has a history of producing huge amount of salts, as well as traditional salted fish and shrimp paste.

Chapter Ten: Off Hong Kong's Beaten Path

Many tourists come to this small but beautiful village primarily because of the Chinese white dolphins that surrounds the area, there were also cultural showrooms and events such as exhibits wherein tourists can learn the fishing history of the village through the relics and old century fishing tools, some of which was donated by the locals.

There are also restaurants and hotels nearby where tourists could stay in and you can also take an exclusive tour along the river through renting boats from the locals for only a small fee.

If you want to go out fishing with the white dolphins, just take the bus 11 going to Tai O bus terminus, the ride will take approximately 50 minutes. Walk to the Rope-drawn Ferry Bridge, it will take you 5 minutes to reach the waterfront. You can also take the MTR Tung Chung Station Exit B. Then you can take the Ngong Ping Cable car to reach the Ngong Ping Village which will take you approximately 25 minutes to get there.

Chapter Ten: Off Hong Kong's Beaten Path

2. Repulse Bay

Repulse Bay is unlike any other beach out there, there's some sort of weird vibe going on in this beach, you can't really tell what it is but once you get there I'm sure you will find out why. Locals and tourists say that this beach is quite mysterious.

It is located in the Southern District of Hong Kong. The history of the bay and how it got its name is also a bit obscure; some locals believe that the bay were used as a base camp of pirates back in the day and they were repulsed by

Chapter Ten: Off Hong Kong's Beaten Path

the Royal Navy, however no historical evidences were found to prove this claim. There were also stories that the bay was named after a ship called HMS Repulse was stationed in the beach, but there are no naval records from the British and even the Chinese navy of such thing. The only record found is from a British admiralty chart but the bay was formerly called the Chonghom Bay. The origin of its name is still unknown.

Around 1910, the bay was developed into a beach, and bus routes were created to attract tourists in Central Hong Kong. During World War II, the Repulse Bay is used as a strategic location. Since the 1860's there were several hotels, shopping malls, restaurants and apartments in the area.

Beach lovers will truly enjoy the clear waters and scenery of this crescent moon shape bay. There are now several resorts that offer lots of beach activities you and your family can enjoy.

To get to the Repulse Bay, take the MTR to Hong Kong station Exit D. At the Exchange Bus Terminal (Central), take the transfer bus 6, 6A, 6X, 66 or 260 which stops at Stanley market and Repulse Bay.

Chapter Ten: Off Hong Kong's Beaten Path

3. Dragon's Back

The Dragon's Back is a place that will satisfy every hikers thirst for adventure and serenity coupled with ancient history. The beautiful coastal scenery and easy accessibility from the city, is a popular escape that is not always included in travel guidebooks.

The trail, a short hop from the bustle of Hong Kong East, provides stunning views of Shek O, Tai Long Wan, Stanley, Tai Tam, and the South China Sea. Reminiscent of the shape of a dragon's backbone, the path of the Dragon's Back undulates between these hilltops which connects

Chapter Ten: Off Hong Kong's Beaten Path

Wan Cham Shan (226m) and Shek O Peak (284m), stretching vertically over D'Aguilar Peninsula. Near to Tei wan village, the entrance to the hike is on Shek O Road. Families as well as solo travelers will surely savor this hike of a lifetime.

4. *Dialogue in the Dark*

If you want to try something cool and "millennial," then Dialogue in the Dark is the best place for yuppies out there and families too!

A world in total darkness, your four senses would take center stage; using only sounds, sense of smell, temperatures and textures. You will have to depend on your

Chapter Ten: Off Hong Kong's Beaten Path

five senses to discover yourself and get through the challenges. Each of the settings will test your sense of touch, hearing, smell, and even sense of taste.

Other activities done in the dark includes the Love Family Experiential Exhibition, Birthday in the Dark, Dinner in the Dark, and Wine Tasting in the Dark. There are also different themes that you could see within the exhibition like a park, a market, a movie theater or a café setting.
Don't worry you will be guided by their visually impaired staff (real blind people) while you're doing all of this cool activities in the dark.

Chapter Ten: Off Hong Kong's Beaten Path

5. *The Beach with the Buffalos*

If you think Repulse Bay is already an interesting island, wait until you see a beach with lots of buffalos! Pui O is the place where you can find the Beach with the Buffalos. It can be seen from the main road along southern Lantau Island. So if you want to swim with these water buffalos, then you better make a stop here.

Nowadays, the old paddy fields which have been abandoned by the farmers are grazing pastures for a few dozen water buffalo. These buffalos seem benign, placid beasts, well used to having people walk and cycle right past them, even though they have huge sizes and gigantic horns. You can only find this kind of beach in Hong Kong!

Chapter Ten: Off Hong Kong's Beaten Path

Aside from the water buffalos, the beach also has magnificent views, and great restaurants surround the area.

For you to get to the Pui O Beach, you could take a ferry from Central Pier 6 to Mui Wo which a fast ferry service would take approximately 35 – 40 minutes in contrast with the ordinary ferry which would take about 50 – 55 minutes. Or you could take the bust to Pui O Beach which the journey would take about just 15 minutes.

Chapter Ten: Off Hong Kong's Beaten Path

6. Mui Wo Clam Digging

If you are not fond of swimming with the buffalos or wearing a bikini then why don't you try clam digging!

Silver mine Bay, or Mui Wo, was the main entry point for Lantau until the advent of Tung Chung New Town. With its beach, hamlets amidst greenery, and two splendid waterfalls, it's definitely one of Hong Kong's off-beaten paths.

The area was a silver mine where many of the inhabitants in the 19th century worked for decades, as its name suggests. The bay has become a swimming beach, though the remnants of the mine can still be seen.

Chapter Ten: Off Hong Kong's Beaten Path

Nowadays, locals and tourists favorite pastime in Mui Wo is clam digging. There are also restaurants by the beach wherein you can rent out clam digging tools and they would even cook your catch for you.

For you to go to Mui Wo, you could take a ferry from Central 6; or a bus 3M from Tung Chung. You could hire a bicycle from near the pier, instead of walking to Mui Wo.

7. Kadoorie Farm

If you like to explore and interact with farm animals that are native in Hong Kong, then the Kadoorie Farm is for you. This farm was originally set up for aiding poor farmers

Chapter Ten: Off Hong Kong's Beaten Path

in the New Territories in Hong Kong, as its former name suggests Kadoorie Experimental and Extension Farm. The promotion of biodiversity conservation in Hong Kong and China, as well as greater environmental awareness is the new focus of this farm. Along with holistic education and practices in support of a transition to sustainable living, it is now managed through an integrated nature conservation, which also includes a rescue and rehabilitation program for native animals.

The founders of the Kadoorie Agricultural Aid Association were The Kadoorie brothers - Lord Lawrence Kadoorie and Sir Horace Kadoorie. They were also the one who planted the seeds for Kadoorie Farm and Botanic Garden. Through training, supply of agricultural inputs and interest-free loans, the aim of the association was to encourage the right mental outlook by helping people to help themselves.

For you to go there you have to take the train, to Kam Sheung Road. Then, get on the 64K bus towards Tai Po. After an extremely steep hill, get off at the Kadoorie Farm bus stop.

Chapter Ten: Off Hong Kong's Beaten Path

8. Mai Po Nature Reserve

If you want to further explore the wilderness of the east, then don't forget to include the Mai Po Nature Reserve on your list. Mai Po Nature Reserve is located near Yuen Long in Hong Kong. It is strategically situated at the mouths of Sham Chun River, Shan Pui River (Yuen Long Creek) and Tin Shui Wai Nullah. The nature reserve is part of a Deep Bay, an internationally significant wetland that is actually a shallow estuary. The Deep Bay supports globally important numbers of wetland birds which is why it is listed as a Ramsar site under Ramsar Convention in 1995; these birds

Chapter Ten: Off Hong Kong's Beaten Path

chiefly arrive in winter and during spring and autumn migrations.

The Agriculture, Fisheries and Conservation Department have responsibilities for the Ramsar site as a whole and the reserve is also managed by the World Wide Fund for Nature Hong Kong since 1983. In recent years, along Deep Bay faces threats, including pollution, climate change and rising mudflat levels that perhaps arise from intense urbanization.

You could take a Minibus No.17 from Shui Che Kwun Street, Yuen Long to Tam Kon Chau Road. After that, take a 20-minute walk to the reserve. Or you could take a KMB Bus No.76K from Long Yat Road near Yuen Long Center to Mai Po Village then after that you would walk towards to the reserve for about 20 minutes.

Chapter Ten: Off Hong Kong's Beaten Path

9. *Hong Kong UNESCO Global Geopark*

Formerly called the Hong Kong National Geopark, the Hong Kong UNESCO Global Geopark was inaugurated on November 3, 2009. Across parts of the Eastern and Northeastern New Territories, it covers an area of 50km. With the combinations of sites, in total it includes over eight sites.

The widely distributed hexagonal rock columns in Sai Kung which have international geological significance and the northeast New Territories region showcasing the complete geological history, which comprises sedimentary rocks formed in different geologic periods, of Hong Kong;

Chapter Ten: Off Hong Kong's Beaten Path

which are the two geological regions of Hong Kong Global Geopark.

Distributed across the Sai Kung Volcanic Rock Region and Northeast New Territories Sedimentary Rock Region, The Geopark is made up of eight Geo-Areas.

For you to go there take MTR University Station, then Exit B and walk about 15 minutes to Ma Liu Shui Landing No.3 to take the ferry to Lai Chi Wo which would take about a 1 hour 30 minutes.

Chapter Ten: Off Hong Kong's Beaten Path

10. Hoi Ha Wan Marine Park

Hoi Ha Wan or Jone's Cove is a marine park in Hong Kong, which is a bay at the north of Sai Kung Peninsula. This is better suited for people who wanted to learn more about marine life and animals around Asia. It is also a hotspot for divers because of its numerous kinds of corals under the sea.

The location has a biological value because it shows significant biodiversity. The park has a sheltered bay with pristine water quality, provides a good marine environment

Chapter Ten: Off Hong Kong's Beaten Path

for housing a great variety of marine organisms. Collecting sea products and corals are prohibited by law.

Fishing, particularly bottom trawling and uses of dynamites or poisons like cyanides which are human intervention are being avoided to keep the local ecosystems pristine condition intact.

For you to go there take the MTR Diamond Hill Station, then exit C2. After that take a 92 or 96R bus (Sunday and public holidays only) to Sai Kung Town, then change to a green minibus 7 to Hoi Ha Tsuen and walk to the Marine Park.

Chapter Ten: Off Hong Kong's Beaten Path

Quick Travel Guide

Can you believe it? You now have all the basic knowledge and idea of what you're going to do when you travel to Hong Kong! I applaud you for finishing this book, now the journey begins!

As discussed here, you can see that Hong Kong is a place full of treasure and beauty. A better way to appreciate it of course is to experience it yourself – experience is a better teacher for sure. Give time and don't pass up this opportunity of a lifetime. You can never experience the fullness of its beauty until you get to see it with your own eyes.

What are you waiting for? I am sure that you are thrilled to explore Hong Kong, but before this comes to an end, here is a quick travel guide. This contains the summary of all the places you've just read through as well as the necessary information that you need while traveling in Hong Kong. Bon Voyage!

1. *Hong Kong Quick Facts*
    a. Currency – Hong Kong dollar (HK$)
    b. Primary Language spoken: Chinese, English
    c. Weather and seasons - unpredictable, but rarely extreme
        - Spring - March, April, to mid-May ; warm, humid with fog and drizzles
        - Summer – May to mid-September, average temperature is 28'C exceeds to 32'C
        - Autumn – September to end of November, cool and dry climate
        - Winter - December, January and February; average of 17'C going down to 10'C
    d. Tourist seasons - pretty much year round, October to September is most

2. Transportation

Points of Entry in Hong Kong

a. Airports
- Hong Kong International Airport
  Ferry Services
- Can be reached from the Chinese mainland water of regular ferries from different terminals located at Macau and Kowloon.

b. By Train
- Victoria Station (from Dover and Newhaven)
- Liverpool Street Station (terminus for Harwich services)
- London Euston Station (links with Holyhead)
- London Paddington Station (interchange at Cardiff Central)

c. By Train
- Through trains are MTR's that runs from Mainland China (Guandong, Shanghai, and Beijing) to Hong Kong.

Transportation Services in Hong Kong

- Taxi
- Ferries
- Airport express
- Buses and minibuses
- MTR
- Trams
- Peak Tram

3. *Travel Essentials*

Immigration and Visas

- For tourists in general, you do not need a visa to enter the city of Hong Kong. Depending on nationality, tourists can stay for 1 up to 180 days without a visa.

Travel Pass for Business Travellers

- This pass is intended to provide business travellers with a simplified and quick immigration procedure as long as they have valid passports and has an entry permit to do business in Hong Kong.

Frequent Visitor e-Channel

- If you would like to always travel to Hong Kong as a tourist, you can also apply for a Frequent Visitor Pass using computerized self-service e-Channels. Acquiring this kind of pass can provide a quick and easy clearance for you or your family at the immigration.

Money Exchange

- Look for a Quality Tourism Services (QTS) Scheme to make sure that the money changer is accredited and safe.

ATMs and Credit Cards

- ATMs are found almost everywhere and are available 24/7.
- You can use international cards and also withdraw to various HSBC 'Electronic Money' machine especially for MasterCard and Visa holders.
- Credit cards such as Visa, MasterCard, American Express and Diners Club are accepted in various hotels, restaurants and shops.

Communication Services

- You can choose between a 5-day pass (HK$90) and 8-day pass (HK$120) tourist sim card. It comes with mobile data for you to have online access that can also have coverage in Mainland China, Macau and Taiwan.
- All you have to do is to open your Wi-Fi, and connect to 'CSL' SSID so that you can have free internet access. It also helps if you download the Wi-Fi HK App so that you have an idea on the location of hotspots in various places.

Reminders and Safety Tips

- Do not leave your valuables unattended. Your money, passport or travel documents should be in a safe place or you should carry it with you at all times.
- Be vigilant and watch out for your valuables especially in crowded places.
- Beware of people offering gambling opportunities or making attempts to distract you and steal your belongings.
- Observe the rules and regulations of public places especially inside shopping malls and tourist spots

Hong Kong Highlights

1.) Must See Temples in Hong Kong

Here's a quick list of the temples you should visit while you are in Hong Kong.

- Po Lin Monastery (Tian Tan Buddha)
- Ten Thousand Buddhas Temple
- Man Mo Temple
- Che Kung Temple
- Chin Lin Nunnery and Nan Lian Garden
- Fung Ying Seen Koon
- Kwan Kung Pavilion
- Seven Sisters Temple
- Golden Flower Shrine
- Hau Wong Temple

2.) Things to do in Hong Kong

Here's a quick list of the things you should experience while you are in Hong Kong.

- Star Ferry Ride
- Duk Ling Ride
- Hong Kong Space Museum
- Hong Kong Cultural Centre
- Lin Heung Tea House

- Madame Tussauds Hong Kong
- Hong Kong Wet Land Park
- Hong Kong Museum of Art
- Yao Ma Tei Theatre
- Arts in the Park Mardi Gras

3.) Night Life in Hong Kong

Here's a quick list of the activities you can do at night time in Hong Kong.

- Symphony of Lights
- Victoria Harbour Cruise
- Aberdeen Harbour Night
- Temple Street Night Market
- Heli-Tour in Hong Kong
- Lan Kwai Fong Bars and Pubs
- Western and Chines Night Clubs
- Happy Valley Racecourse
- Opera Hong Kong
- Intercontinental Infinity Pools

4.) Off Hong Kong's Beaten Path

Here's a quick list of the unchartered places you should explore in Hong Kong.

- Tai O Fishing Village
- Repulse Bay
- Dragon's Back
- Dialogue in the Dark
- The Beach with the Buffalo
- Mui Wo Clam Digging
- Kadoorie Farm
- Mai Po Nature Reserve
- Hong Kong Unseco Global Geopark
- Hoi Ha Wan Marine

PHOTO REFERENCES

Page 1 Photo by skeeze via Pixabay

<https://pixabay.com/en/hong-kong-harbor-night-lights-city-561246/>

Page 5 Photo by Unsplash via Pixabay

<https://pixabay.com/en/hong-kong-cityscape-1209806/>

Page 6 Photo by Unsplash via Pixabay

<https://pixabay.com/en/hong-kong-china-night-cityscape-1081704/>

Page 11 Photo by TravelCoffeeBook via Pixabay

<https://pixabay.com/en/pagoda-temple-asia-religion-594585/>

Page 16 Photo by Christian Bélanger via Flickr

<https://www.flickr.com/photos/krissserz/14297584148/in/photolist-nMqRDw>

Page 17 Photo by J Aaron Farr via Flickr

<https://www.flickr.com/photos/jaaronfarr/519948326/>

Page 32 Photo by ShenXin via Pixabay

<https://pixabay.com/en/hong-kong-street-view-central-1886027/>

Page 43 Photo by Russell_Yan via Pixabay

<https://pixabay.com/en/hong-kong-skyline-night-urban-1763063/>

Page 45 Photo by DesignerPoint via Pixabay

<https://pixabay.com/en/hong-kong-peek-night-long-exposure-1791067/>

Page 47 Photo by johnlsl via Flickr

<https://www.flickr.com/photos/johnlsl/20438835954/>

Page 49 Photo by Pexels via Pixabay

<https://pixabay.com/en/hong-kong-sailing-ship-sea-1836843/>

Page 51 Photo by Charlotte Powell via Flickr

<https://www.flickr.com/photos/14545665@N04/5302626407/in/photostream/>

Page 53 Photo by johnlsl via Flickr

<https://www.flickr.com/photos/johnlsl/21927416371/>

Page 55 Photo by Gonzalo Pineda Zuniga via Flickr

<https://www.flickr.com/photos/gonzo_pz/10280103926/>

Page 57 Photo by Martin Lewison via Flickr

<https://www.flickr.com/photos/milst1/12044146154/>

Page 59 Photo by Marc van der Chijs via Flickr

<https://www.flickr.com/photos/chijs/49032613/>

Page 61 Photo by Andy Enero via Flickr

<https://www.flickr.com/photos/andyenero/8278160506/>

Page 62 Photo by Paul Frankenstein via Flickr

<https://www.flickr.com/photos/frankenstein/16526900433/>

Page 64 Photo by Unsplash via Pixabay

<https://pixabay.com/en/asian-cuisine-food-meal-dinner-872118/>

Page 65 Photo by CarpLei via Wikimedia Commons

<https://commons.wikimedia.org/wiki/File:HK_Causeway_Bay_Tang_Lung_Street_Restaurants_1.JPG>

Page 67 Photo by KLN CT via Wikimedia Commons

<https://commons.wikimedia.org/wiki/File:HK_Kln_City_Nga_Tsin_Wai_Road_near_Hoover_Cafe_n_Jewelry_Shop.JPG>

Page 68 Photo by Nicolas Vollmer via Wikimedia Commons

<https://commons.wikimedia.org/wiki/File:Nathan_Road_(8613257863).jpg>

Page 70 Photo by Stewart via Wikimedia Commons

<https://commons.wikimedia.org/wiki/File:Lan_Kwai_Fong_Carnival_-_2007-10-12_19h06m20s_SN203590.JPG>

Page 72 Photo by Terence Ong via Wikimedia Commons

<https://commons.wikimedia.org/wiki/File:Canton_Road_2.JPG>

Page 73 Photo by Mandralimari via Wikimedia Commons

<https://commons.wikimedia.org/wiki/File:HK_Hung_Hom_%E7%B4%85%E7%A3%A1_%E5%AF%B6%E5%85%B6%E5%88%A9%E8%A1%97_Bulkeley_Street_temple_Mar-2013.JPG>

Page 75 Photo by Ángel Riesgo Martínez via Wikimedia Commons

<https://commons.wikimedia.org/wiki/File:Hong_Kong_de_noche.jpg>

Page 76 Photo by Hoi Shing WANG via Wikimedia Commons

<https://commons.wikimedia.org/wiki/File:HK_%E4%B9%9D%E9%BE%8D%E5%9F%8E_Kln_City_%E9%BE%8D%E5%B4%97%E9%81%93_Lung_Kong_Road_Feb-2014_Prince_Ritz_sidewalk_shop_McDonalds.JPG>

Page 77 Photo by Fahad Faisal via Wikimedia Commons

<https://commons.wikimedia.org/wiki/File:Stanley_Road_food_court.JPG>

Page 79 Photo by Typhoonchaser via Wikimedia Commons

<https://commons.wikimedia.org/wiki/File:Fishmongers_in_Sai_Kung_2.JPG>

Page 81 Photo by bichvn via Pixabay

<https://pixabay.com/en/ocean-hong-kong-sea-1068294/>

Page 82 Photo by nate2b via Flickr

<https://www.flickr.com/photos/napdsp/10161056266/>

Page 84 Photo by Niall Kennedy via Flickr

<https://www.flickr.com/photos/niallkennedy/2547496827/>

Page 86 Photo by hhyunma via Pixabay

<https://pixabay.com/en/hong-kong-ocean-park-the-cable-car-1100890/>

Page 88 Photo by cotaro70s via Flickr

<https://www.flickr.com/photos/cotaro70s/17928750262/>

Page 89 Photo by IQRemix via Flickr

<https://www.flickr.com/photos/iqremix/9454511368/>

Page 90 Photo by Jennifer Morrow via Flickr

<https://www.flickr.com/photos/donotlick/4219225389/>

Page 92 Photo by Andrew and Annemarie via Flickr

<https://www.flickr.com/photos/andrew_annemarie/14350530192/>

Page 94 Photo by buttermia via Pixabay

<https://pixabay.com/en/car-%E7%BA%9C-hong-kong-high-altitude-711429/>

Page 97 Photo by (WT-ja) Tatata via Wikimedia Commons

<https://commons.wikimedia.org/wiki/File:HK_Golden_Bauhinia_Square.JPG>

Page 98 Photo by Eugene Lim via Flickr

<https://www.flickr.com/photos/eugenelimphotography/14866822920/>

Page 101 Photo by Jens Schott Knudsen via Flickr

<https://www.flickr.com/photos/pamhule/8088630012/>

Page 102 Photo by Chris Chu via Flickr

<https://www.flickr.com/photos/cchu/3031426493/>

Page 104 Photo by jennandion via Flickr

<https://www.flickr.com/photos/jennandjon/11575494326/>

Page 106 Photo by Bevis Chin via Flickr

<https://www.flickr.com/photos/bionikk1/11286997113/>

Page 108 Photo by roaming-the-planet via Flickr

<https://www.flickr.com/photos/roaming-the-planet/6698492203/>

Page 110 Photo by Stephen Kelly via Flickr

<https://www.flickr.com/photos/skellysf/6993281287/>

Page 112 Photo by Sue Prasetio via Flickr

<https://www.flickr.com/photos/soe_the_arts/7748089168/>

Page 114 Photo by Matt Mayer via Wikimedia Commons

<https://commons.wikimedia.org/wiki/Category:Kwan_Kung_Pavilion#/media/File:Cheung_chau_temple.jpg>

Page 115 Photo by Chong Fat via Wikimedia Commons

<https://commons.wikimedia.org/wiki/File:HK_PengChau_Seven_Sisters_Temple.JPG>

Page 117 Photo by thetempletrail via Flickr

<https://www.flickr.com/photos/89356268@N08/20107308972/>

Page 119 Photo by SpirosK photography via Flickr

<https://www.flickr.com/photos/spirosk/2808421631/>

Page 121 Photo by Mitch Altman via Flickr

<https://www.flickr.com/photos/maltman23/6909078122/>

Page 122 Photo by Bernard Spragg.NZ via Flickr

<https://www.flickr.com/photos/volvob12b/15853925347/>

Page 125 Photo by bomb_bao via Flickr

<https://www.flickr.com/photos/bomb_bao/4143854950/in/photolist>

Page 127 Photo by Tiny House Brewing & Farmstead's Photostream via Flickr

<https://www.flickr.com/photos/95875907@N04/16787155850/>

Page 128 Photo by See - ming Lee via Flickr

<https://www.flickr.com/photos/seeminglee/8405001913/>

Page 130 Photo by Chelsea Marie Hicks via Flickr

<https://www.flickr.com/photos/seafaringwoman/6635200991/>

Page 132 Photo by Shinya Ichinohe via Flickr

<https://www.flickr.com/photos/shinyai/5350208789/>

Page 134 Photo by 巴黎 陳 via Flickr

<https://www.flickr.com/photos/pallaschan/2265486056/>

Page 136 Photo by Tracy Hunter via Flickr

<https://www.flickr.com/photos/tracyhunter/8533681401/>

Page 137 Photo by IMjust86 via Wikimedia Commons

<https://commons.wikimedia.org/wiki/File:The_3D_TV_cinema.JPG>

Page 138 Photo by Hong Kong Tourism Board via DiscoverHongKong.com

<http://www.discoverhongkong.com/ca/see-do/arts-performance/highlight-events/arts-in-the-park-mardi-gras.jsp>

Page 140 Photo by chiaoyinanita via Pixabay

< https://pixabay.com/en/sparks-fire-light-rotation-flames-265850/>

Page 141 Photo by Daniel Go via Flickr

<https://www.flickr.com/photos/danielygo/14322785558/>

Page 143 Photo by Ed Coyle via Flickr

<https://www.flickr.com/photos/joxur223/5759960917/>

Page 145 Photo by John Allan via Wikimedia Commons

<https://commons.wikimedia.org/wiki/File:Aberdeen_Harbour_-_geograph.org.uk_-_330872.jpg>

Page 147 Photo by kartografia via Flickr

<https://www.flickr.com/photos/kartografia/2744546640/>

Page 149 Photo by Christian Junker Photography via Flickr

<https://www.flickr.com/photos/chrisjunker/4683840663/in/photolist-88TUDv-KoDcZ>

Page 150 Photo by Chris via Flickr

<https://www.flickr.com/photos/desdegus/3376825204/>

Page 152 Photo by Mitch Lorens via Flickr

<https://www.flickr.com/photos/mlorens/2287137086/>

Page 153 Photo by johnlsl via Flickr

<https://www.flickr.com/photos/johnlsl/16276112207/>

Page 155 Photo by Henry Wang via pixabay.com

<https://pixabay.com/en/hong-kong-central-night-view-958778/>

Page 157 Photo by InterContinental Hong Kong via Flickr

<https://www.flickr.com/photos/intercontinentalhongkong/10940472033/>

Page 159 Photo by ImageDragon via Pixabay

<https://pixabay.com/en/old-buildings-residential-area-1415534/>

Page 160 Photo by Bill Hertha via Flickr

<https://www.flickr.com/photos/whertha/2609666280/>

Page 162 Photo by Bertrand Duperrin via Flickr

<https://www.flickr.com/photos/beberonline/15615762710/>

Page 164 Photo by Mark Lehmkuhler via Flickr

<https://www.flickr.com/photos/mark_lehmkuhler/4883712083/>

Page 165 Photo by king jai via Flickr

<https://www.flickr.com/photos/king318/7196329738/>

Page 167 Photo by joensch via Wikimedia Commons

<https://commons.wikimedia.org/wiki/File:Buffalo.JPG>

Page 169 Photo by David Bailey via Flickr

<https://www.flickr.com/photos/davidbaileymbe/3518924630/>

Page 170 Photo by chailey via Flickr

<https://www.flickr.com/photos/chailey/496056329/>

Page 172 Photo by Lip Jin Lee via Flickr

<https://www.flickr.com/photos/levoodoo/4028931351/>

Page 174 Photo by Keith Au via Flickr

<https://www.flickr.com/photos/110203569@N03/11290362153/>

Page 176 Photo by Chong Fat via Wikimedia Commons

<https://commons.wikimedia.org/wiki/File:HK_HoiHaWanMarinePark.JPG>

Page 178 Photo by tpsdave via Pixabay

<https://pixabay.com/en/hong-kong-city-urban-skyscrapers-1990268/>

REFERENCES

"5 Things to Do to Make the Most of Your Stopover Time in Hong Kong" China Highlights

<http://www.chinahighlights.com/hong-kong/article-things-to-do-stopover.htm>

"9 Things to do in Lantau Island Hong Kong" TopOnMyList.com

<http://www.toponmylist.com/9-things-to-do-in-lantau-island-hongkong/>

"10 Things to Know Before You Visit Hong Kong" LittleGreyBox

<https://littlegreybox.net/2015/05/19/10-things-to-know-before-you-visit-hong-kong/>

"12 Things to do in Ngong Ping" Virtual Tourist

<https://www.virtualtourist.com/travel/Asia/Hong_Kong/Ngong_Ping-1083287/Things_To_Do-Ngong_Ping-TG-C-1.html>

"20 Things to do in Hong Kong" Fodor's Travel

<http://www.fodors.com/world/asia/china/hong-kong/experiences/news/photos/20-ultimate-things-to-do-in-hong-kong>

"24 Things You Should Do When Visiting Hong Kong" Business Insider

<http://www.businessinsider.com/best-things-to-do-in-hong-kong-2015-2>

"10,000 Buddhas Monastery" LonelyPlanet.com

<https://www.lonelyplanet.com/china/hong-kong/attractions/10-000-buddhas-monastery/a/poi-sig/1245466/1001879>

"A Beginner's Guide to Hong Kong: Causeway Bay" HK Travel 360

<https://hktravel360.wordpress.com/2013/02/14/causeway-bay/>

"Aberdeen & Harbour Night" Discover Hong Kong

<http://www.discoverhongkong.com/seasia/see-do/tours-walks/guided-tours/night/aberdeen-harbour-night.jsp>

"A Day Trip to Lamma Island" Hong-Kong-Traveller

<http://www.hong-kong-traveller.com/lamma-island.html#.WIrnl9J97Dc>

"Admiralty, Central and SoHo" Discover Hong Kong

<http://www.discoverhongkong.com/seasia/shop/where-to-shop/shopping-areas/admiralty-central-soho.jsp>

"Airport Express" Discover Hong Kong

<http://www.discoverhongkong.com/ca/plan-your-trip/traveller-info/transport/getting-around/airport-express.jsp>

"Applying Visa" Discover Hong Kong

<http://www.discoverhongkong.com/ca/plan-your-trip/traveller-info/immigration-and-customs/applying-visa.jsp>

"Arts in the Park Mardi Gras" Discover Hong Kong

<http://www.discoverhongkong.com/seasia/see-do/arts-performance/highlight-events/arts-in-the-park-mardi-gras.jsp>

"A Symphony of Light" Travel China Guide

<https://www.travelchinaguide.com/attraction/hongkong/symphony-of-lights.htm>

"A Symphony of Light" Wikipedia.org

<https://en.wikipedia.org/wiki/A_Symphony_of_Lights>

"Avenue of Stars" HongKongExtras.com

<http://www.hongkongextras.com/_avenue_of_stars.html>

"A Victoria Harbour Cruise" Hong-Kong-Traveller

<http://www.hong-kong-traveller.com/victoria-harbour-cruise.html>

"Best Restaurants near Percival Street" Yelp.com

<https://www.yelp.com/search?find_desc=Restaurants&find_loc=1%2FF%2C60+Percival+Street%2CCausewaybay%2CHK%2C+Hong+Kong>

"Best Things to do in Hong Kong" U.S. News

<http://travel.usnews.com/Hong_Kong_China/Things_To_Do/>

"Buses and Minibuses" Discover Hong Kong

<http://www.discoverhongkong.com/ca/plan-your-trip/traveller-info/transport/getting-around/buses-and-minibuses.jsp>

"Central, Hong Kong" Wikipedia.org

<https://en.wikipedia.org/wiki/Central,_Hong_Kong>

"Central Hotels" Trip Advisor

<https://www.tripadvisor.com.ph/Hotels-g294217-zfn7350425-Hong_Kong-Hotels.html>

"Che Kung Temple at Sha Tin" Discover Hong Kong

<http://www.discoverhongkong.com/seasia/see-do/culture-heritage/chinese-temples/che-kung-temple-at-sha-tin.jsp>

"Che Kung Miu" Wikipedia.org

"https://en.wikipedia.org/wiki/Che_Kung_Miu"

"Chi Lin Nunnery and Nan Lian Garden" Discover Hong Kong

<http://www.discoverhongkong.com/seasia/see-do/culture-heritage/chinese-temples/chi-lin-nunnery-and-nan-lian-garden.jsp>

"Chi Lin Nunnery and Nan Lian Garden" NextStopHongKong

<http://www.nextstophongkong.com/chi-lin-nunnery-and-nan-lian-garden/>

"Climate" Discover Hong Kong

<http://www.discoverhongkong.com/eng/plan-your-trip/traveller-info/about-hong-kong/climate.jsp>

"Clock Tower Hong Kong" NextStopHongKong.com

<http://www.nextstophongkong.com/clock-tower/>

"Customs" Discover Hong Kong

<http://www.discoverhongkong.com/ca/plan-your-trip/traveller-info/immigration-and-customs/customs.jsp>

"Dialogue in the Dark" ChinaTravel.com

<http://www.chinatravel.com/hong-kong-attraction/dialogue-in-the-dark/>

"Dialogue in the Dark" Discover Hong Kong

<http://www.discoverhongkong.com/seasia/see-do/culture-heritage/museums/special-interests/dialogue-in-the-dark.jsp>

"Dragon's Back Trail, Hong Kong Island" Walking English Man

<http://www.walkingenglishman.com/world01.html>

"Duk Ling – Enjoying an Authentic Chinese Junk Ride in Hong Kong Victoria Harbour" NextStopHongKong

<http://www.nextstophongkong.com/duk-ling-enjoying-an-authentic-chinese-junk-ride-in-hong-kong-victoria-harbor/>

"East of Eden: With Kayak and Snorkel to Far-Flung Hong Kong" CNN Travel

<http://travel.cnn.com/hong-kong/visit/kayaking-under-sea-hoi-ha-wan-279964/>

"Electricity and Voltage" Discover Hong Kong

<http://www.discoverhongkong.com/ca/plan-your-trip/traveller-info/good-to-know/electricity-and-voltage.jsp>

"Ferries" Discover Hong Kong

<http://www.discoverhongkong.com/ca/plan-your-trip/traveller-info/transport/getting-around/ferries.jsp>

"Fly and Dine" The Peninsula Hong Kong

<http://hongkong.peninsula.com/en/special-offers/fly-and-dine>

"Fung Ying Seen Koon" Trip Advisor

<https://www.tripadvisor.com.ph/Attraction_Review-g294217-d7146398-Reviews-Fung_Ying_Seen_Koon-Hong_Kong.html>

"Fung Ying Seen Koon" Wikipedia.org

<https://en.wikipedia.org/wiki/Fung_Ying_Seen_Koon>

"Golden Bauhinia Square" Wikipedia.org

<https://en.wikipedia.org/wiki/Golden_Bauhinia_Square>

"Golden Flower Shrine" Discover Hong Kong

<http://www.discoverhongkong.com/seasia/see-do/culture-heritage/chinese-temples/golden-flower-shrine.jsp>

"Golden Flower Shrine – A Colorful Temple in Peng Chau Hong Kong" IloveHongKong

<http://ilovehongkong.org/golden-flower-shrine-peng-chau-hong-kong/>

"Guide to Visiting Hong Kong's Big Buddha and Po Lin Monastery" LaJollaMom.com

<http://lajollamom.com/big-buddha-po-lin-monastery/>

"Hau Wong Temple" Discover Hong Kong

<http://www.discoverhongkong.com/seasia/see-do/culture-heritage/chinese-temples/hau-wong-temple.jsp>

"Happy Valley Hong Kong" Hong-Kong-Traveller

<http://www.hong-kong-traveller.com/happy-valley-hong-kong.html#.WIskkNJ97Dc>

"Happy Valley Racecourse" Wikipedia.org

<https://en.wikipedia.org/wiki/Happy_Valley_Racecourse>

"Hau Wong Temple in Tung Chung" Itishk.com

<http://www.itishk.com/hau-wong-temple-in-tung-chung/>

"Health and Safety" Discover Hong Kong

<http://www.discoverhongkong.com/ca/plan-your-trip/traveller-info/good-to-know/health-and-safety.jsp>

"Heli-Tour of Hong Kong" Time.com

<http://content.time.com/time/travel/cityguide/article/0,31489,1850110_1850124_1850912,00.html>

"Hoi Ha Wan Marine Park" Discover Hong Kong

<http://www.discoverhongkong.com/seasia/see-do/great-outdoors/nature-parks/hoi-ha-wan-marine-park.jsp>

"Hoi Ha Wan Marine Park – Snorkeling in Hong Kong" Visions of Travel

<http://www.visionsoftravel.org/hoi-ha-wan-marine-park-snorkeling-in-hong-kong/>

<http://www.visionsoftravel.org/hoi-ha-wan-marine-park-snorkeling-in-hong-kong/>

"Hoi Ha Wan Marine Park: Snorkel + Kayak + Beach" LittleStepsAsia.com

<http://www.littlestepsasia.com/hong-kong/articles/play/hoi-ha-wan-marine-park>

"Hong Kong" Wikipedia.org

<https://en.wikipedia.org/wiki/Hong_Kong>

"Hong Kong" EveryCulture.com

<http://www.everyculture.com/Ge-It/Hong-Kong.html>

"Hong Kong, China" TripAdvisor.com.ph

<https://www.tripadvisor.com.ph/Tourism-g294217-Hong_Kong-Vacations.html>

"Hong Kong Culture" Travel China Guide

<https://www.travelchinaguide.com/cityguides/hongkong/when-to-go.htm>

"Hong Kong Cultural Centre" Discover Hong Kong

<http://www.discoverhongkong.com/seasia/see-do/arts-performance/arts-venues/hong-kong-cultural-centre.jsp>

"Hong Kong Cultural Centre" Wikipedia.org

<https://en.wikipedia.org/wiki/Hong_Kong_Cultural_Centre>

"Hong Kong Disneyland" Wikipedia.org

<https://en.wikipedia.org/wiki/Hong_Kong_Disneyland>

"Hong Kong Disneyland – Top 10 Attractions" Discover Hong Kong

<http://www.discoverhongkong.com/seasia/see-do/highlight-attractions/top-10/hong-kong-disneyland.jsp>

"Hong Kong Global Geopark" Wikipedia.org

<https://en.wikipedia.org/wiki/Hong_Kong_Global_Geopark>

"Hong Kong Guide" Commisceo-Global.com

<http://www.commisceo-global.com/country-guides/hong-kong-guide>

"Hong Kong Museum of Art" Fodors.com

<http://www.fodors.com/world/asia/china/hong-kong/things-to-do/sights/reviews/hong-kong-museum-of-art-419706>

"Hong Kong Museum of Art" Wikipedia.org

<https://en.wikipedia.org/wiki/Hong_Kong_Museum_of_Art>

"Hong Kong Museum of History" Hong-Kong-Traveller

<http://www.hong-kong-traveller.com/hong-kong-museum-of-history.html#.WIsOzdJ97Dc>

"Hong Kong: Need to Know" Time.com

<http://content.time.com/time/travel/cityguide/article/0,31489,1850110_1851057_1851058,00.html>

"Hong Kong NightLife" TravelChinaGuide.com

<https://www.travelchinaguide.com/cityguides/hongkong/nightlife.htm>

"Hong Kong Profile – Timeline" BBC.com

<http://www.bbc.com/news/world-asia-pacific-16526765>

"Hong Kong Space Museum" Wikipedia.org

<https://en.wikipedia.org/wiki/Hong_Kong_Space_Museum>

"Hong Kong Space Museum" NextStopHongKong.com

<http://www.nextstophongkong.com/hong-kong-space-museum/>

"Hong Kong Transportation" Travel China Guide

<https://www.travelchinaguide.com/cityguides/hongkong/transportation/>

"Hong Kong Transportation: By Air, Sea, Train, Tram, MTR and Taxi" Chinahighlights.com

<http://www.chinahighlights.com/hongkong/transportation.htm>

"Hong Kong Travel Guide" Chinahighlights.com

<http://www.chinahighlights.com/hong-kong/>

"Hong Kong Travel Guide" TravelChinaGuide.com

<https://www.travelchinaguide.com/cityguides/hongkong/>

"Hong Kong UNESCO Global Geopark"
Discover Hong Kong

<http://www.discoverhongkong.com/seasia/see-do/great-outdoors/nature-parks/hong-kong-unesco-global-geopark.jsp>

"Hong Kong's Victoria Peak" Hong Kong Traveller

<http://www.hong-kong-traveller.com/victoria-peak.html#.WIsMPdJ97Dc>

"Hong Kong Weather Guide" TravelChinaGuide.com

<https://www.travelchinaguide.com/climate/hongkong.htm>

"Hong Kong's Wetland Park" Hong Kong Extras

<http://www.hongkongextras.com/_hong_kong_wetland_park.html>

"Hong Kong's Wetland Park" Wikipedia.org

"https://en.wikipedia.org/wiki/Hong_Kong_Wetland_Park"

"Hotels near to Causeway Bay" Hotels.com

<https://ph.hotels.com/nh851/hotels-in-causeway-bay-hong-kong-hong-kong/>

"Hotels near Lantau Island" Trip Advisor

<https://www.tripadvisor.com.ph/HotelsNear-g294217-d447109-Lantau_Island-Hong_Kong.html>

"Hotels near to Mong Kok" Hotels.com

<https://ph.hotels.com/nh1645229/hotels-in-mong-kok-hong-kong-hong-kong/>

"Hotels near to Hong Kong Sheung Wan Station" Hotels.com

<https://ph.hotels.com/de1724132/hotels-near-hong-kong-sheung-wan-station-sheung-wan-hong-kong/>

"Hotels near to Stanley Main Beach" Hotels.com

<https://ph.hotels.com/de1660769/hotels-near-stanley-main-beach-hong-kong-hong-kong/>

"Hotels near to Wan Chai" Hotels.com

<https://ph.hotels.com/nh1645215/hotels-in-wan-chai-hong-kong-hong-kong/>

"How to get to Avenue of Stars" The Poor Traveler

<http://www.thepoortraveler.net/2013/08/tsim-sha-tsui-to-avenue-of-stars-directions-walking-hong-kong/>

"How to Spend a Night in Hong Kong" ChinaHighlights.com

<http://www.chinahighlights.com/hong-kong/nightlife.htm>

"How to Visit Big Buddha in Hong Kong" Travelling9to5.com

<http://www.traveling9to5.com/2012/01/how-to-visit-the-big-buddha-hong-kong/>

"History" Discover Hong Kong

<http://www.discoverhongkong.com/uk/plan-your-trip/traveller-info/about-hong-kong/history.jsp>

"Immigration" Discover Hong Kong

<http://www.discoverhongkong.com/ca/plan-your-trip/traveller-info/immigration-and-customs/immigration.jsp>

"Infinity Pool at InterContinental Hong Kong" FroschInsider.com

<http://froschinsider.com/infinity-pool-at-intercontinental-hong-kong/>

"Jumbo Floating Restaurant" Hong-Kong Traveller

<http://www.hong-kong-traveller.com/jumbo-floating-restaurant.html#.WIsOENJ97Dc>

"Kadoorie Farm & Botanic Garden" Discover Hong Kong

<http://www.discoverhongkong.com/seasia/see-do/great-outdoors/nature-parks/kadoorie-farm-botanic-garden.jsp>

"Kadoorie Farm, New Territories" HKOutdoors.com

<http://www.hkoutdoors.com/new-territories/kadoorie-farm.html>

"Kwan Kung Pavillion" IloveHongKong

<http://www.ilovehongkong.hk/hong-kong/things-do/kwan-kung-pavilion>

"Kwan Kung Pavillion" Wikipedia.org

<https://en.wikipedia.org/wiki/Kwan_Kung_Pavilion>

"Language and Culture" Discover Hong Kong

<http://www.discoverhongkong.com/ca/plan-your-trip/traveller-info/about-hong-kong/language-and-culture.jsp>

"Lantau's Island Big Buddha: Is It Worth It?" A Cruising Couple

<http://acruisingcouple.com/2013/06/lantau-island-hong-kong-is-the-big-buddha-worth-it/>

"Lantau Island Attractions and Day Trips" Hong-Kong Traveller

<http://www.hong-kong-traveller.com/lantau-island-attractions.html#.WIrm99J97Dc>

"Lin Heung Tea House" Foodie Topography

<http://foodietopography.net/lin-heung-tea-house/>

"Lin Heung Tea House" Time.com

<http://content.time.com/time/travel/cityguide/article/0, 31489, 1850110_1850124_1850300, 00.html>

"Lung Kong Road" Openrice.com

<https://www.openrice.com/en/hongkong/restaurants?where=Lung%20Kong%20Road&page=1>

"Madame Tussauds" NextStopHongKong

<http://www.nextstophongkong.com/madame-tussauds/>

"Madame Tussauds" Travel China Guide

<https://www.travelchinaguide.com/attraction/hongkong/madame-tussauds.htm>

"Man Mo Temple" Wikipedia.org

<https://en.wikipedia.org/wiki/Man_Mo_Temple_(Hong_Kong)>

"Mai Po Nature Reserve" Discover Hong Kong

<http://www.discoverhongkong.com/seasia/see-do/great-outdoors/nature-parks/mai-po-nature-reserve.jsp>

"Mai Po Nature Reserve" Hong-Kong Traveller

<http://www.hong-kong-traveller.com/mai-po-nature-reserve.html#.WIspUtJ97Dc>

"Money" Discover Hong Kong

<http://www.discoverhongkong.com/ca/plan-your-trip/traveller-info/good-to-know/money.jsp>

"MongKok Hong Kong" hk-mongkok.com

<http://www.hk-mongkok.com/>

"MTR" Discover Hong Kong

<http://www.discoverhongkong.com/ca/plan-your-trip/traveller-info/transport/getting-around/mtr.jsp>

"Mui Wo: An Island Getaway in Hong Kong" RoundWorldTravels.com

<http://www.roundworldtravels.com/mui-wo-an-island-getaway-in-hong-kong/>

"Nga Tsin Wai" OpenRice.com

<https://www.openrice.com/en/hongkong/restaurants?ST=1&region=0&has_coupon=1&where=nga+tsin+wai>

"Ngong Ping 360" Discover Hong Kong

<http://www.discoverhongkong.com/seasia/see-do/great-outdoors/outlying-islands/lantau-island/ngong-ping-360.jsp>

"Ngong Ping 360" Wikipedia

<https://en.wikipedia.org/wiki/Ngong_Ping_360>

"Ocean Park Hong Kong" Wikipedia.org

<https://en.wikipedia.org/wiki/Ocean_Park_Hong_Kong>

"Ocean Park Hong Kong – Top 10 Attractions" Discover Hong Kong

<http://www.discoverhongkong.com/seasia/see-do/highlight-attractions/top-10/ocean-park-hong-kong.jsp>

"Octopus Card" Discover Hong Kong

"http://www.discoverhongkong.com/ca/plan-your-trip/traveller-info/transport/getting-around/octopus-card.jsp"

"Off the Beaten Track" EducationPost.com

<http://www.educationpost.com.hk/resources/parents-guide/140526-family-fun-off-the-beaten-track>

"Opera Hong Kong" Discover Hong Kong

<http://www.discoverhongkong.com/seasia/see-do/arts-performance/performing-companies/opera-hong-kong.jsp>

"Peng Chau, Hong Kong's Underdog Island" CNN Travel

<http://travel.cnn.com/hong-kong/play/peng-chau-hong-kongs-most-underrated-island-escape-510599/>

"Peng Chau Hotels" Hotels.com

<https://ph.hotels.com/de605494/hotels-peng-chau-hong-kong/>

"Po Lin Monastery" Wikipedia.org

<https://en.wikipedia.org/wiki/Po_Lin_Monastery>

"Public Holidays" Discover Hong Kong

<http://www.discoverhongkong.com/ca/plan-your-trip/traveller-info/good-to-know/public-holidays.jsp>

"Pui O, Lantau Island" HKOutdoors.com

<http://www.hkoutdoors.com/lantau-island/pui-o-lantau.html>

"Quick Guide to Hong Kong's Great Outdoors" UniGlobe One Travel

<http://www.uniglobeonebc.com/post/view/quick-guide-to-hong-kong-s-great-outdoors>

"Repulse Bay" Travel China Guide

<https://www.travelchinaguide.com/attraction/hongkong/island/bay.htm>

"Repulse Bay" Wikipedia.org

<https://en.wikipedia.org/wiki/Repulse_Bay>

"Restaurants near Canton Road" Trip Advisor

<https://www.tripadvisor.com.ph/RestaurantsNear-g294217-d2226357-Canton_Road-Hong_Kong.html>

"Restaurants near Lan Kwai Fong" Trip Advisor

<https://www.tripadvisor.com.ph/RestaurantsNear-g294217-d603110-Lan_Kwai_Fong_Hotel-Hong_Kong.html>

"Restaurants near Nathan Road" Trip Advisor

<https://www.tripadvisor.com.ph/RestaurantsNear-g294217-d537986-Nathan_Road-Hong_Kong.html>

"Sailing on a Hong Kong Junk" Hong-Kong Traveller

<http://www.hong-kong-traveller.com/hong-kong-junk.html#.WIsaodJ97Dc>

"Seven Sisters Temple" Discover Hong Kong

<http://www.discoverhongkong.com/seasia/see-do/culture-heritage/chinese-temples/seven-sisters-temple.jsp>

"Seven Sisters Temple" Green Peng Chau

<http://greenpengchau.org.hk/theme.php?page_id=Temp7Sister&lang=e>

"Sheung Wan" Wikipedia.org

<http://www.discoverhongkong.com/seasia/shop/where-to-shop/shopping-areas/sheung-wan.jsp>

"Sightseeing in Hong Kong: The Dragon Back Hiking Trail" Adventures of Anette

<http://adventuresofanette.blogspot.com/2015/05/sightseeing-in-hong-kong-dragon-back.html>

"Standard Chartered Arts in the Park Mardi Gras" Hong Kong Youth Arts Foundation

<http://www.hkyaf.com/category/6/standard-chartered>

"Stanley" Hong-Kong-Traveller

<http://www.hong-kong-traveller.com/lamma-island.html#.WIrnl9J97Dc>

"Star Ferry" Discover Hong Kong

<http://www.discoverhongkong.com/seasia/see-do/highlight-attractions/harbour-view/star-ferry.jsp>

"Star Ferry" Time

<http://content.time.com/time/travel/cityguide/article/0,31489,1850110_1850124_1850920,00.html>

"Star Ferry" Wikipedia.org

<https://en.wikipedia.org/wiki/Star_Ferry>

"Tai O Fishing Village" Hong-Kong-Traveller

<http://www.hong-kong-traveller.com/tai-o-fishing-village.html>

"Tai O – Fishing Village" NextStopHongKong

<http://www.nextstophongkong.com/tai-o-fishing-village/>

"Tang Lung Restaurants" OpenRice.com

<https://www.openrice.com/en/hongkong/restaurants?where=tang%20lung%20street>

"Taxi" Discover Hong Kong

<http://www.discoverhongkong.com/ca/plan-your-trip/traveller-info/transport/getting-around/taxi.jsp>

"Temple Street Market" ChinaHighlights.com

<http://www.chinahighlights.com/hong-kong/attraction/temple-street-market.htm>

"Temple Street Night Market" Hong-Kong-Traveller

<http://www.hong-kong-traveller.com/temple-street-night-market.html#.WIsiTdJ97Dc>

"Ten Thousand Buddhas Monastery" NextStopHongKong.com

<http://www.nextstophongkong.com/10000-buddha-temple/>

"Time is Running out Fast for Hong Kong's Water Buffalo" South China Morning Post

<http://www.scmp.com/magazines/post-magazine/article/1849170/time-running-out-fast-hong-kongs-water-buffalo>

"Top 10 things to do in Hong Kong" China Highlights

<http://www.chinahighlights.com/hong-kong/top-things-to-do.htm>

"Touring Victoria Harbour" Discover Hong Kong

<http://www.discoverhongkong.com/seasia/see-do/tours-walks/guided-tours/victoria-harbour/index.jsp>

"The 10 Best Restaurants in Stanley Hong Kong" The Culture Trip

<https://theculturetrip.com/asia/hong-kong/articles/the-10-best-restaurants-in-stanley-hong-kong/>

"The Beach with the Buffalo Hong Kong" Inside the Travel Lab

<http://www.insidethetravellab.com/the-beach-with-the-buffalo-hong-kong/>

"The Best Alternative Things to do in Hong Kong" Culture Trip

<https://theculturetrip.com/asia/hong-kong/articles/top-14-alternative-things-to-do-in-hong-kong/>

"The Best Bars in Lan Kwai Fong" Go Hong Kong

<http://gohongkong.about.com/od/hongkongbarsandclubs/ss/lankwaifongpubs.htm>

"The Best Restaurants in Sai Kung" TimeOut.com

<https://www.timeout.com/hong-kong/restaurants/the-best-restaurants-in-sai-kung>

"The Dragon's Back and beyond: The Best Hikes in Hong Kong" Lonely Planet

<https://www.lonelyplanet.com/china/hong-kong/travel-tips-and-articles/the-dragons-back-and-beyond-the-best-hikes-in-hong-kong>

"The Hong Kong Museum of History" Discover Hong Kong

<http://www.discoverhongkong.com/seasia/see-do/culture-heritage/museums/history/museum-of-history.jsp>

"The Peak Tram" Discover Hong Kong

<http://www.discoverhongkong.com/ca/plan-your-trip/traveller-info/transport/getting-around/the-peak-tram.jsp>

"The Top 10 Things to See and Do in Tsim Sha Tsui, Hong Kong" Culture Trip

<https://theculturetrip.com/asia/hong-kong/articles/the-top-10-cultural-things-to-do-and-see-in-tsim-sha-tsui/>

"Things to Do near Butao Ramen(Tang Lung Street)"

Trip Advisor

<https://www.tripadvisor.com.ph/AttractionsNear-g294217-d4474105-Butao_Ramen_Tang_Lung_Street-Hong_Kong.html>

"Trams" Discover Hong Kong

<http://www.discoverhongkong.com/ca/plan-your-trip/traveller-info/transport/getting-around/trams.jsp>

"Travel Insurance" Discover Hong Kong

"http://www.discoverhongkong.com/ca/plan-your-trip/traveller-info/travel-insurance.jsp"

'Tsim Sha Tsui" Wikipedia.org

<https://en.wikipedia.org/wiki/Tsim_Sha_Tsui>

'Tsim Sha Tsui" TravelChinaGuide.com

<https://www.travelchinaguide.com/attraction/hongkong/kowloon/tsim_sha.htm>

'Tsim Sha Tsui Clock Tower" Hong Kong Trip Guide

<http://www.hongkongtripguide.com/tsim-sha-tsui-clock-tower.html>

"Victoria Harbour" Wikipedia.org

<https://en.wikipedia.org/wiki/Victoria_Harbour>

"Victoria Harbour: Hong Kong's Prized Landmark" Hong-Kong Traveller

<http://www.hong-kong-traveller.com/victoria-harbour.html#.WIsRdNJ97Dc>

"Victoria Peak – A Breathtaking Bird's Eye View in Hong Kong" Chinahighlights.com

<http://www.chinahighlights.com/hong-kong/attraction/victoria-peak.htm>

"Wanchai" TravelChinaGuide.com

<https://www.travelchinaguide.com/attraction/hongkong/island/wanchai.htm>

"Wan Chai" Wikipedia.org

<https://en.wikipedia.org/wiki/Wan_Chai>

"What Are Some Things to Know Before Visiting Hong Kong" ForbesTravelGuide.com

<http://www.forbestravelguide.com/hong-kong-china/what-are-some-things-to-know-before-visiting-hong-kong>

"What's Up with the Buffaloes on Lantau Island" CNN Travel

<http://travel.cnn.com/hong-kong/life/whats-buffaloes-lantau-739010/>

"Yau Ma Tei Theatre" Discover Hong Kong

<http://www.discoverhongkong.com/seasia/see-do/arts-performance/arts-venues/yau-ma-tei-theatre.jsp>

Feeding Baby
Cynthia Cherry
978-1941070000

Axolotl
Lolly Brown
978-0989658430

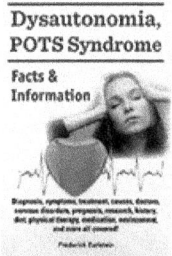

Dysautonomia, POTS Syndrome
Frederick Earlstein
978-0989658485

Degenerative Disc Disease Explained
Frederick Earlstein
978-0989658485

Sinusitis, Hay Fever,
Allergic Rhinitis Explained
Frederick Earlstein
978-1941070024

Wicca
Riley Star
978-1941070130

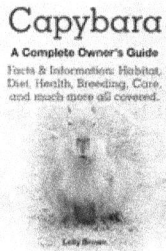

Zombie Apocalypse
Rex Cutty
978-1941070154

Capybara
Lolly Brown
978-1941070062

Eels As Pets
Lolly Brown
978-1941070167

Scabies and Lice Explained
Frederick Earlstein
978-1941070017

Saltwater Fish As Pets
Lolly Brown
978-0989658461

Torticollis Explained
Frederick Earlstein
978-1941070055

Kennel Cough
Lolly Brown
978-0989658409

Physiotherapist, Physical Therapist
Christopher Wright
978-0989658492

Rats, Mice, and Dormice As Pets
Lolly Brown
978-1941070079

Wallaby and Wallaroo Care
Lolly Brown
978-1941070031

Bodybuilding Supplements
Explained
Jon Shelton
978-1941070239

Demonology
Riley Star
978-19401070314

Pigeon Racing
Lolly Brown
978-1941070307

Dwarf Hamster
Lolly Brown
978-1941070390

Cryptozoology
Rex Cutty
978-1941070406

Eye Strain
Frederick Earlstein
978-1941070369

Inez The Miniature Elephant
Asher Ray
978-1941070353

Vampire Apocalypse
Rex Cutty
978-1941070321

www.ingramcontent.com/pod-product-compliance
Lightning Source LLC
Chambersburg PA
CBHW071657090426
42738CB00009B/1561